LAUNCH

LIFE SCIENCES PRODUCTS

The leading practical guide to life sciences launch success.

David Bard, MBA | Canadian Edition

Canadian Edition

© 2014 by David M. Bard

ISBN 978-0-9938510-0-1

Published 2014 by Life Sciences Publishing

Designed by Kristen Clancy of Red Pencil Design

*This book is dedicated to my mother, **Ann R. Bard**,*
a woman who always stood firmly for her beliefs.

CONTENTS

STRATEGIC DECISION POINT 2: DEVELOP THE PRODUCT

STRATEGIC CHECK-IN POINT 6:
LAUNCH EFFECTIVENESS

Author's Launch Insights

Launch: Life Sciences Products was written based on my personal observations and experience, starting as an associate product manager, when I noticed early on that my manager, who was recruited for his launch experience, actually had no formal launch process. Soon after starting as the launch lead, the manager spent time developing list after list of launch tasks.

This is not an anomaly: most of the organizations I worked with throughout my commercial career had no formal process for a launch. Typically, companies select a talented individual from marketing to lead the commercial launch, based on his or her experience and success on a prior launch. That individual then creates multiple worksheets filled with checklists in an attempt to capture the extensive list of tasks required for launch. In researching this book, I interviewed corporate executives from a number of companies. Each one identified a similar haphazard launch process, wherein a marketer with launch experience was recruited and left to identify the timeline and tasks required for a particular product launch. This was true across North America regardless of company size.

My intention with this book was to develop a list of all the potential tasks associated with any life sciences product launch to save companies' time, money and the pain of potential task omissions. If nothing else, this book is a comprehensive checklist to kick off your new product launch.

When one considers the size of an investment to acquire or to develop a new asset, I am still puzzled as to why smart businesspeople do not invest more in launch process development.

PREFACE

Life sciences companies have never faced more challenges than they do today when launching new products into the market. To be successful, product launches must be carefully planned and flawlessly executed. Only then can the launch gain sales uptake momentum, demonstrate superior product performance and offer greater cost efficiencies. The trend towards cost efficiency in this market intensifies the importance of delivering maximum value to customers, as well as to the company, with each new product formulation or indication launch.

Despite attempts to build an effective product launch process, many companies struggle to get it right, which can significantly impact the company's bottom line and future success. The ability of life sciences companies to implement a well-established and effective launch process and/or to address and overcome existing corporate launch weaknesses can mean the difference between a company and its products succeeding in the market, floundering, or fading away.

In this book, David Bard presents his comprehensive thirty-six month guide to launch success which spans the planning, launch execution and post-launch assessment phases of the process. Bard's book provides a step-by-step guide – a detailed road map to a successful life sciences product launch that will enable organizations to transform their launch performance.

A product launch comprises the planning and execution of product development and commercialization activities in order to introduce a new product or indication to the market. The commercial launch period begins with the licensing of new technology or even in the early stages of clinical development for proprietary products. For the purposes of this framework, the launch period is defined as the span that begins twenty-four months prior to notice of compliance (NOC) and ends twelve months after the market introduction of the product; it may run parallel to the implementation of subsequent product life cycles, such as the launch of a new formulation or additional indications.

Bard has outlined an end-to-end product launch process along six launch stages, each of which consists of several major steps required for success. Product launches must include research, analysis, planning and execution of the product's development and commercialization.

The first three stages center on planning and development:
1. Planning and developing the company.
2. Planning and developing the product.
3. Planning and developing the market.

The final three stages can be considered strategic check-in points:
4. Launch readiness review.
5. The launch.
6. Launch effectiveness.

This six-stage process can be performed on a global and local level. The strategic differences in process will be determined by the scope of activities from a global perspective.

Product launches are complex projects due to global and local alignments and the involvement of cross-functional teams. To be able to master this complexity and achieve high performance in a product launch, the following five key components are required:

1. A clear new product launch process that is comprehensive, flexible and adaptable. It must include strong leadership and clearly defined roles for each team member. Finally, all activities must be mapped to a timeline that is monitored to ensure critical milestones are achieved.

2. A comprehensive launch commercial plan with deep and robust customer and market insights, as well as clear and focused choices. These will help develop credible and meaningful strategies and ensure sustainable competitive advantage based on customer needs.

3. Organizational alignment, engagement, excitement and execution of the commercial opportunity. Upper management must be committed to and engaged in the product launch to drive internal awareness and excitement.

4. Launch communication including clear objectives, clear measurement tools and dashboard performance: A good launch process celebrates the wins and rapidly addresses the gaps.

5. Financial resources to support the level of product launch needed for success. Identification of the launch priority within the organization and ensuring appropriate measurement to enable a comprehensive review of product launch performance.

Author's Launch Insights

At the outset of a gastrointestinal drug launch, the entire company received a clear message from the president about the importance of the product in question. It was critical that all internal work requests related to this product were to be the highest priority, as this launch was the organization's main objective. As a result of the company-wide priority placed on the launch, multiple records were broken and new launch capabilities sprung up throughout the organization.

Figure 1 – New Product Launch Framework

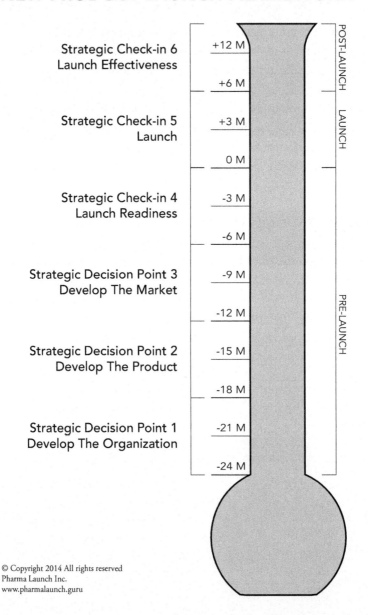

STRATEGIC DECISION & CHECK-IN POINTS
NEW PRODUCT LAUNCH FRAMEWORK

Strategic Check-in 6 Launch Effectiveness	+12 M
	+6 M
Strategic Check-in 5 Launch	+3 M
	0 M
Strategic Check-in 4 Launch Readiness	-3 M
	-6 M
Strategic Decision Point 3 Develop The Market	-9 M
	-12 M
Strategic Decision Point 2 Develop The Product	-15 M
	-18 M
Strategic Decision Point 1 Develop The Organization	-21 M
	-24 M

POST-LAUNCH

LAUNCH

PRE-LAUNCH

Figure 1 – New Product Launch Framework

A market assessment was conducted to identify Canadian best-in-class product launches. Several IMS reports were reviewed, including the 2007 and 2008 special reports, entitled Defining Global Launch Excellence. Additional content was provided by area experts, who offered their recommendations regarding best-in-class launch requirements. The launch timelines and associated key tasks were provided by the author, based on more than ten successful life sciences product launches. The *Launch: Life Sciences Products* manuscript was reviewed by qualified experts to refine the new product launch (NPL) process.

The author hopes that you find the information in this book useful. By following the steps outlined herein, we are certain that you will see a positive impact on your products, services, and overall revenues.

The New Product Launch Framework was created to communicate a launch process in a visual way. The Framework identifies the six stages of a launch; outlines six key decision points; identifies workflow team involvement, and provides a simple means to communicate the progress achieved, corporate-wide.

INTRODUCTION TO NEW PRODUCT LAUNCH PLANNING

Life sciences companies face incredible challenges when they launch new products today. For example, intense generic competition commences after patent expiry, which causes significant value erosion. Consequently, it is essential to maximize product value during patent protection and to consider life cycle management strategies early in a product's development. Furthermore, patent expiry and weak pipelines enhance the need to optimize replacement pipeline product sales. This, in turn, creates the need for successful new product launches.

Current requirements, standards and market trends have created a number of implications for life sciences companies, many of which can hinder successful launches, validating the absolute necessity of creating an effective launch process. One such difficulty is the increased focus on in-licensing, which requires the development of new capabilities and improved flexibility to quickly ramp up resources to launch in-licensed products. Another possible barrier to launch success is a change in sales models, which creates a need for the effective coordination of resources.

Externally, poor public perception can magnify the need to initiate positive reception of both new products and life sciences organizations. Payor and authority figures have been under pressure, making the demonstration of superior product value a requirement, not a bonus.

To respond effectively to these dynamics, life sciences companies need to maximize product launch capabilities. They must also accelerate launch uptake to offset sales gaps resulting from patent expiry, and maximize sales throughout the patent-protected product life cycle. The key areas to fine tune include cost, patents, market access and individual and team capabilities.

LAUNCH Life Sciences Products provides a detailed how-to guide for the comprehensive product launch process. This guide was developed to answer the need for an established process to launch new life sciences products into the Canadian marketplace. In his experience, the author noted that few companies, regardless of size, had an established launch process, a significant lack given that the launch is always key for a company to successfully introduce their significant investments into the marketplace. This guide provides information on the requisite tasks for all members of a product launch team and will be useful company-wide.

Launch Excellence Defined

The lack of a launch process is the most obvious factor that may hinder launch success – important steps can be overlooked or taken too late. Unfortunately, assessments of past errors often do not provide enough concrete information to prepare well for the next launch opportunity.

This launch process model differs from others because it offers clear, comprehensive information for all team members in all stages of the operation.

Because companies experience continual churn due to promotions, lateral moves and recruitment to new organizations, their launch capabilities often migrate with the employees who change positions as part of their career progressions. That's why it's essential to build both individual and corporate launch capabilities by developing a standardized, yet flexible launch process, which this guide does.

Four key elements make a process successful:
1. **Transparency** – to be capable of identifying required activities and their measurement criteria. This allows for evaluation at all critical decision points of the process.

2. **Clarity** – an outsider unfamiliar with the project should be able to understand it. Such clarity leads to better decision-making and fulfillment of responsibilities.

3. **Predictability** – every possible outcome should be anticipated. As a process develops, identifying possible outcomes and their probabilities on a process map allows for time to prepare for every outcome.

4. **Efficiency** – the resources both consumed and produced in the launch process should be the minimum necessary to achieve the desired outcome.

Benefits of a Product Launch Process

Simply put, a sound product launch process enhances a company's launch capabilities, accelerating its advance to high performance. In the early days and during the post-launch stage, a review of past product launches is recommended to identify where improvements can be made and which processes should be continued.

An important question to consider is: how successful were your organization's prior product launches? Data tells us that most product launches are met with mixed success. Examine past launches for: time to market; time to first sale, post-notice of compliance; uptake within first six months of launch, and several other key metrics, such as total prescriptions from first sale onward.

A quality launch process offers tools that help companies coordinate complex, multi-country launches by following consistent processes across all locations.

Few companies have a process that will accommodate different types of launches: new chemical entities, line-extensions and licensed products in late

Stage III clinical research. The approach shared here recognizes that each product acquisition is unique and may require a different launch strategy. Gantt charts accompany the reference guide, which can be purchased from the author, based on two very different product launch types: new chemical entity (NCE)/reformulation and currently marketed drug acquisitions. This new product launch process provides detailed information on all the metrics and considerations to assess previous product launches and shows companies how to use what they learn to accelerate growth and achieve desired performance.

Author's Launch Insights

During a consulting assignment, a client asked me to review his company's launch capability for timing to market. I forecasted a loss of sales based on the number of days late to market for five brands. Each brand was late to market by 45–165 days, and the total loss tallied more than $160 million. Many consulting firms can provide a thorough review of past launch performance to ensure that effective processes are maintained and that processes which require improvement are identified.

The Launch Process

The new product launch process is intended to guide teams through multiple stages of launch preparation and assessment, focusing on coordinated efforts to gain faster regulatory approvals, rapid market access and expedited product availability. In addition, this process is designed to enhance any pharmaceutical company's core competency in launching new products to best-in-class status.

With the excitement of a blockbuster launch and direct communication from our CEO to make the new gastrointestinal drug a priority company-wide, this directive created a tremendous amount of support, yet it also created conflict regarding human resources allocation. Managing expectations is key to maintaining morale. Team members need to be identified and well informed, so everyone understands when and how they are expected to work on a new product's development. Develop a clear process with role clarity and clear timelines.

New Product Launch Planning

New Product Launch Planning, often referred to as "NPLP," is conducted at the development stage, and takes into consideration the full cycle of the product's life. Life Cycle Management (LCM) models include five stages:

> **Stage 1:** Development/Prelaunch
> **Stage 2:** Launch/Introduction
> **Stage 3:** Growth
> **Stage 4:** Maturity
> **Stage 5:** Decline

Here are key questions that should be asked during new product launch planning:

- What are the key challenges in the launch space?
- What are the windows of opportunity?
- What are the pitfalls of various strategies?
- What are the roles of the cross-functional team and engaged stakeholders?
- How will medical affairs play an increasingly important role in product launches?

This guide provides a comprehensive list of tasks, as well as explanations for initial planning and development stages. The launch process stages are explained in the following section.

Product Launch Process Stages

The launch process spans thirty-six months: it begins twenty-four months prior to approval or receipt of notice of compliance (NOC) and ends twelve months post launch.

The process is divided into six organized stages:
    Stage 1: Developing the Company
    Stage 2: Developing the Product
    Stage 3: Developing the Market
    Stage 4: Launch Readiness
    Stage 5: Launch
    Stage 6: Launch Assessment

These six stages are allotted time frames, with key tasks identified within each stage. The time frames can be readily associated with more detailed Gantt charts. Key responsibilities, expected output and recommendations are provided for every step of the process. To further assist the launch process, examples and tables have been provided.

Product Launch Process Framework

Each stage will begin with a table outlining required tasks that need to be taken. After each table, individual tasks are explained in detail and include:

1. Associated teams responsible for the execution of the task.
2. Specific output sought.
3. Detailed planning recommendations.

Each stage is designed to provide an overview of key areas for development and launch check-in points. Please note that this process, as with any process, requires refinement based on your company's specific needs and the needs of the ever-changing life sciences marketplace. Although presented chronologically, some development tasks may need to be initiated sooner than specified, depending on the product's key issues or strategies. It should be noted that many activities are initiated at an early stage and will carry on throughout the launch.

Prepare, Prepare, Prepare

The key to launch excellence is preparation. While working through *Launch: Life Sciences Products,* refer to the action guides and checklists that correspond with each launch stage. These guides and checklists help the team prepare for the launch and enable cross-team efficiency, while facilitating updates to senior management. There is a section at the end of each stage for notes.

The teams that must execute specific tasks and coordinate other tasks are described in the References section. Additional material in the Appendix can assist Market Access and Regulatory teams.

This book can acts as a guide as each stage is completed, as a book of standards for launch team members to follow, and even as a workbook. It is recommended that key team members read through the entire launch process to determine where variation may be needed.

Who Should Read This Book

All life sciences employees should read this book, particularly all members supporting a launch:
- CEO, GM, VPs.
- All product launch teams.

- Marketing and brand management.
- Regulatory, Quality Assurance, Sales, Supply, Market Access, Medical Affairs and Market Research.
- Any commercial agency supporting a launch including advertising agencies, public relations agencies, market analytics firms, key opinion leaders, and other consultants.

The Excitement Begins

Launching a new pharmaceutical product is a fast-paced, challenging and highly exciting project to lead. It is extremely satisfying to look back on the success of a launch and reflect on the impact it made on the health and well-being of potentially thousands of patients. When a brand launch succeeds and makes a significant financial contribution to an organization, the thrill is real. When preparing to launch a drug, the launch team leadership must envision the brand performing at a higher level than a typical launch and never settle for second best.

- Launch diagnostics for best-in-class preparation.
- Planning to ensure adequate resourcing and flawless execution.
- Key performance indicators for consistent tracking of launch success.
- Launch excellence across regions.
- Better launch planning across all functions: marketing, sales, regulatory, training, medical, and market access teams.

The excitement of a launch begins in the initial planning stages and builds from there. An effective launch process removes the need to monitor hundreds of tasks, thus strengthening an organization's capabilities and ensuring launch readiness. After the launch, process evaluation will help to improve the performance of future product launches, paving the way for life sciences companies to become high-performance entities.

STRATEGIC DECISION POINT 1:
DEVELOP THE ORGANIZATION

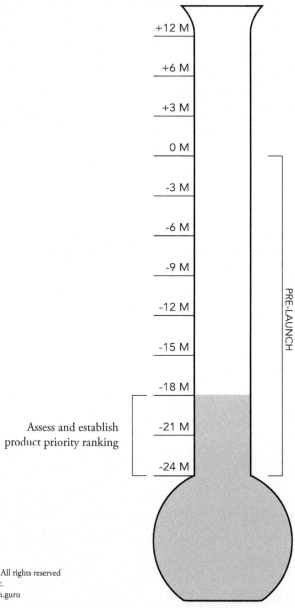

+12 M

+6 M

+3 M

0 M

-3 M

-6 M

-9 M

-12 M

-15 M

-18 M

Assess and establish
product priority ranking

-21 M

-24 M

PRE-LAUNCH

STRATEGIC DECISION POINT 1: DEVELOP THE ORGANIZATION

The key questions to answer at Strategic Decision Point 1 are:
1. How large is this opportunity?
2. How many resources do we invest?
   - Rank new product priority.
   - Build a launch team.
   - Communicate the importance of the product within the organization.
   - Complete the regulatory review of the file.
   - Assess favourable pricing alternatives.
   - Assess and establish brand priority ranking.

Tasks Initiated at Twenty-Four Months Pre-Launch

Every product launch brand has the potential to achieve world-class status. However, without careful preparation, any launch brand can end in failure. The mantra of Pfizer, a Top-10 pharmaceutical company, is "Blockbusters are made," which is entirely true, as is the reverse.

The launch team must rely on the product they are commercializing as it impacts customers' understanding of it, the payor's willingness to pay for it, and the patient's willingness to consume it. Without thoughtful preparation in the twenty-four months prior to launch, gaps in key areas will prevent the product from achieving peak sales.

The first decision point in the framework involves developing the company, when it decides how to resource the branding appropriate to the size of the opportunity. At this decision point, the team completes a commercial assessment of the opportunity and identifies the product's key issues. The team then provides senior management with a ranking assessment, such as an "A," "B" or "C" brand priority. An "A" brand represents a large opportunity, whereas a "C" brand would represent a lesser opportunity but still be financially viable.

The team involved in this stage consists of: GM, Regulatory, Finance, Marketing, Legal, Market Access and Market Research.

Strategic Decision Point 1 requires a detailed commercial assessment to establish the company's brand priority ranking, crucial to prioritize it amongst other projects. An "A" brand, for example, would be given top priority for internal resources, whereas a "C" brand might receive a smaller budget and more external resources. Brands may change rankings over time as new information become available. A brand's ranking should not impact the quality of the preparation for the launch. Decision criteria are provided below for all rankings.

The purpose of ranking brands is to ensure that resources are assigned appropriately according to the magnitude of the business opportunity. A company may have to stretch its personnel and finances if it has too many brands competing for its limited resources. Failing to establish priorities may prevent a company from reaching launch excellence for any of its brands. Lower brand rankings may still be vitally important to the company, but they require different skills and tools to achieve success, such as the use of contracted or partner resources.

By ranking product priority for each product's development, an optimal structure is established. As a general rule, structure follows strategy.

Table 1: Brand ranking criteria

Brand Ranking Criteria	A	B	C
Market Size	Large	Medium	Small
Product Profile Attractiveness	High	Moderate to High	Moderate
Five Year Net Present Value (NPV) (in millions)	> $150 M	> $75 M	> $25M

Cost of Entry	Acceptable	Acceptable	Acceptable
Corporate Priorities	Strong Fit	Good Fit	Marginal Fit

Author's Launch Insights

While launching three brands simultaneously in an organization, determining launch priorities became a challenge. When we assessed the products from a strategic perspective and their contribution to the organization's specialty focus versus simply the financial contribution on an annual basis, priorities became clearer. Two brands were aligned with our corporate specialty focus and a third brand was offering primary care a superior treatment – a one-off product! As a result, it did not deserve the same resources as products aligned with the corporation's specialty area. Ultimately, despite a lower priority, the primary care product still became the number one treatment within its therapeutic area.

The table on the following page lists the tasks that need to be performed in the earliest launch stage, with a primary focus on developing the company. Each task will be covered in detail in this section. The table lists the groups that are chiefly responsible for implementing each task. The last column provides the timeline outlining when each task should be initiated.

Table 2: Summary of tasks at twenty-four months pre-launch

Item	Task	Responsibility	Timeline
1	Establish Product Launch Planning Team	Leadership Team	L–24 months
2	Assess Inventory of Global Launch Resources	General Manager	L–24 months
3	New Drug Submission (NDS) Guidance	Regulatory	L–24 months
4	Product Monograph Development	Team	L–23 months

5	Create Finance Project Number and Expense Budgets	Finance	L–23 months
6	Intellectual Property: Confirm, Compound and Formulate Patents	Legal	L–23 months
7	Product Trademarks, Branding and Naming	Legal	L–22 months
8	Establish Key Launch Milestones	Area Leads / NPL Team	L–22 months
9	Common Drug Review Consultation	Market Access	L–22 months
10	Develop and Initiate Market Research Plan	Market Research	L–22 months
11	Detailed Initial Commercial Assessment	NPP	L–21 months
12	Corporate-wide Launch Awareness	Marketing	L–20 months
13	Pricing Strategy: Pricing and Market Access Plan	NPL Team	L–20 months

The following section provides detailed information on the recommended tasks required to develop the company to achieve launch excellence.

Task 1:
Establish Product Launch Planning Team

Responsibility for Decision: Corporate Leadership Team
Output: Establish the core cross-functional launch team.

Planning Recommendations:

The first step in the launch process is the kick-off meeting during which senior management introduces team members and their primary responsibilities. At this meeting, the newly created, cross-functional New Product Launch (NPL) team will assess the tasks to be initiated and enlist the appropriate stakeholders for each task. An important step in launch team development is to communicate early when new members will join the team.

The six-stage strategic decision and check-in points provide an excellent overview to inform team members at which point(s) their expertise will be required, which will help to motivate them as they are well informed.

Successful product development demands a cross-functional approach beginning in the earliest, pre-clinical stages prior to the product's transfer to new product marketing. Early-stage commercialization staff often participates in teams with business development, research and development (R&D), medical affairs, regulatory, legal, clinical, supply and others. A list of these teams and their functions will be covered below and can be found in the Appendix. Cross-functional product development processes ensure that decisions are well thought out and that checks and balances are in place as perspectives from across the company are included.

Within the NPL team, a product manager is responsible for the short- and long-term profitable progress of the brand in the marketplace through effective planning, execution, control and training. Regulatory is responsible for all activities involving the submission and receipt of approval from Therapeutic Product Directorate (TPD). Finance is responsible for all financial statements and budgetary controls. Supply and quality assurance (QA) are responsible for providing the final product for sale that meets good manufacturing practices (GMP). Market access is responsible for gaining approval on formularies to allow the brand to reach its fullest potential. Finally, legal is responsible for ensuring that contract provisions, trademarks and patents are in place to maximize the product's life cycle.

Initially, keep the cross-functional launch team small. Include only the individuals required at each stage of development, using the checklists provided at the beginning of each stage. Multiple ad hoc teams can be formed beyond the core team for specific short- and long-term projects. Meetings should be scheduled monthly or bi-weekly in the beginning to facilitate the flow of information and expedite product planning. Each area of the launch team should be responsible for writing its section of the plan.

To give a product the best chance at long-term success, priority must be given to developing the launch team. When considering a product's launch and life cycle, solicit input from all functional areas, whether your organization establishes a cross-functional NPL team or passes responsibilities from function to function. Functional ownership may actually speed decisions. Cross-functional launch team collaboration ensures access to the knowledge and experience of multiple divisions and departments.

Task 2:
Assess Inventory of Global Launch Resources

Responsibility for Decision: General Manager and Business Development Team
Output: Key files and documents are made available to new product launch (NPL) team.

Planning Recommendations:

Once the transfer of the new product from the business development team is completed, the commercial team (including the NPL team) has the "green light" to begin planning. Whether the new product is an acquired product or developed within the company, the business development team has invested considerable resources into its assessments, thus a thorough review of all business development files is warranted to quickly augment the commercial team's familiarity with the product. The NPL team needs access to the due diligence process files, key assumptions, forecasts, commercial plans, pivotal clinical trials, partner agreement (which includes term sheets), the international launch sequence, international pricing guidelines, conditions, Therapeutic Product Directorate (TPD) file status, product supply lead times, branding and trademark information, Intellectual Property (IP), market research and Life Cycle Management (LCM) plans.

Business development assessments are essential to understanding the opportunity presented to the NPL team and serve as a fast-track foundation for effective planning. They provide an invaluable perspective on the product's potential in the market.

Author's Launch Insights

The transfer of all files from the business development team is important to understand the product's development, anticipated market opportunities and licensing arrangements. It is also important for the business development team to assess the priorities of all development brands. In one organization, the business development leader believed that sharing the product files would not allow the product development team to develop its own ideas for the brand, but contributing to product development ought to be an organization-wide initiative. Gaining perspective from all team members will broaden a product's strategic options and make a product more successful.

Task 3:
New Drug Submission (NDS) Guidance

Responsibility for Decision: Regulatory
Output: Plan and execute pre-NDS meeting and follow-up with Therapeutic Product Directorate (TPD) for clinical program and submission guidance.

Planning Recommendations:

To give a new product its best chance at success, a focused effort on rapid approval from TPD is paramount. *The NDS submission is the most important part of the launch. Without a timely submission, review and approval, the product does not launch.*

The groundwork for the NDS must be meticulous in every way; all information and documentation must be assembled as required by the TPD with extreme diligence. Key components include: efficacy and safety, chemistry and manufacturing, non-clinical and clinical data. The pre-clinical stage of research initiates prior to clinical trials, to demonstrate drug safety. The clinical trials focus on testing the drug in humans.

There are few hard and fast rules for NDS development, but some pertinent guidelines may help facilitate preparation. TPD Guidelines can be obtained through the Health Canada Website: **www.hc-sc.gc.ca/dhp-mps/prodpharma/applic-demande/index-eng.php** or directly from TPD, Bureau of Pharmaceutical Assessment, Finance Building, Tunney's Pasture, Ottawa, Ontario, K1A 1B6.

Before NDS preparation begins, determine if FDA or ICH guidelines may be relevant to the NDS. In some cases, the U.S. Food and Drug Administration (FDA) has more regulatory guidelines than does TPD. These should be reviewed for relevance. The International Conference on Harmonization (ICH) is working to standardize regulatory requirements in Europe, Japan and the U.S. and TPD has adopted these guidelines. Prior to moving too far ahead in the NDS's development, a pre-NDS meeting with the reviewers at TPD is common.

Prepare a pre-meeting package containing a summary of all clinical and technical data to be used in the preparation of the NDS. Members of the regulatory and medical teams present the data that will be submitted to support the NDS. Outstanding issues or concerns raised by the reviewing unit can be clarified and negotiated at the meeting

Task 4: Product Monograph Development

Responsibility for Decision: Regulatory, NPP, Medical and Marketing
Output: A product monograph (PM) is aligned with commercialization objectives.

Planning Recommendations:

Development of a well-crafted product monograph is critical to a product's success since the wording in the product monograph influences the degree of success or failure for a new product. Make all attempts to include relevant information including key disease and brand messages in the product monograph because it is essential for future promotional purposes.

The responsibility for NDS preparation resides with the regulatory and medical teams with input from New Product Planning (NPP) and marketing teams in regards to the information that is critical to the new product's ability to compete.

Prior to preparing the product monograph, assess competitor products for class labelling guidelines that may apply directly to the new product. Review competitive monographs for style and content, especially those that provide the specific products' competitive advantages. All product monograph statements and claims must be supported in the submission by literature and data. Failure to provide sufficient support may delay approvals. Another valuable suggestion is to gain Key Opinion Leader (KOL) perspectives on the key drivers of prescribing within the product's treatment area, as well as to include product differentiation in order to support future promotional efforts. A recommendation is to hire a consultant to provide a competitive product monograph review. The person developing the product monograph review needs a strategic skill set to recognize competitive promotional opportunities and the long term promotional environment in Canada. The product monograph is the most important competitive document in the product's life cycle.

A well-referenced product monograph is vital to a product's promotional success. Be sure to look five to ten years down the road to determine where your product's promotional opportunities lie. To achieve this objective, use an outside marketing consultant with both regulatory and commercialization expertise for an in-depth competitive product monograph assessment and review.

Task 5:
Create Project Number & Expense Budgets

Responsibility for Decision: Finance
Output: Set up a project number for the product, as well as the preliminary expense budget and budget codes.

Planning Recommendations:

It is financially prudent to establish a project number to efficiently track expenses. When the product is transferred from business development to the launch team, it is important to calculate the preliminary expense estimates for the next three to six months. A project number, set up with your financial partner and all launch team members, will track the product expenses. Although actual product codes will eventually be created, all expenses in the short-term need to be allocated to a project number for streamlined organization. It is recommended to involve your financial team early as key partners in the product's development.

Task 6:
Intellectual Property: Confirm Compound, Formulation Patents & Distribution Rights

Responsibility for Decision: Legal and Cross-functional Team
Output: Patent review for intellectual property (IP).

Planning Recommendations:

File applications for patents early to protect market exclusivity. As part of the business opportunity review, include a review of the patent standing for the new product, whether it is an in-house R&D or a licensing opportunity.

Some key points to consider:
- Review Orange Book to verify any patent registration numbers, and, where required, report on any patent information received from licensing partners.
- All dosages and formats used in any clinical trials must be patent-protected.
- Confirm the patent status with your company patent agents.
- Patents related to a new medicine should also be registered with Health Canada. This step is not mandatory but should be considered as a deterrent to premature generic applications. It is recommended to register all issued patents with Health Canada when the NDS is submitted for review.
- Be certain to verify if there are any competitive patents that should concern your company.

Both compounds and formulations must carry patents. At this stage, the active pharmaceutical ingredient (API) or compound for the new product should already have a registered patent. Health Canada maintains a patent register, linked to Notices of Compliance, forcing any generic manufacturer to notify the patent holder by way of Notice of Allegation (NOA), prior to filing an abbreviated new drug submission. The innovator can then institute court proceedings to prevent the issuance of an NOC to the generic manufacturer while the patent is in place. Strict conditions apply to the entry of a patent on Health Canada's register.

When patents are registered, the legal team should verify that:
- Only patents for a medicine or use of a medicine can be registered (chemical process patents cannot be registered with Health Canada).
- All inventions relating to the product are the subject of patent applications filed before the NDS is made.
- All issued patents must be submitted for registration at the same time as the NDS.
- All patents relating to the product must be re-submitted for registrations whenever a supplemental NDS is made.
- Any new patents issued after submitting the NDS must be submitted for registration within thirty days of their issuance.

The IP status defines the lifecycle timeframe of the brand. Several intellectual patent claims exist, such as:

Claim for the medicinal ingredient – is made in the patent, whether chemical or biological in nature, when it has been prepared or produced by the methods or processes of manufacture that are described and claimed in the patent or by their obvious chemical equivalents. It also includes a claim for different polymorphs of the medicinal ingredient, but does not include different chemical forms of the medicinal ingredient.

Claim for the formulation – a claim for a substance that is a mixture of medicinal and non-medicinal ingredients in a drug that is administered to patients in a particular dosage form.

Claim for the dosage form – a claim for a delivery system for the administration of a medicinal ingredient in a drug or a formulation of a drug that includes within its scope that medicinal ingredient or formulation.

Claim for the use of the medicinal ingredient – a claim for the use of the ingredient for the diagnosis, treatment, mitigation or prevention of a disease, disorder or abnormal physical state or for its symptoms.

An example of a patent claim summary is provided in the table below for Product X.

Table 3 – Patent claim summary

PATENT #	CLAIM
1000011	Product – An orally administrable controlled release composition comprising a pharmaceutically acceptable form of product X.
1000012	Delivery–An extended-release galenical composition of one or more pharmaceutically acceptable salts of product X.
1000013	Controlled Release Layer

Distribution rights for a licensed product define the geographical territory for sales and marketing of a product. Understanding constraints is important, such as a stipulation on number of calls annually.

Task 7:
Product Trademarks, Branding & Naming

Responsibility for Decision: Legal, Business Development, Regulatory and NPP
Output: Brand name established, trademarks identified and registered.

Planning recommendations:

Be sure to use the appropriate trademarks on all promotional materials. All trademarks should be clearly identified with the **TM** symbol. Once registered, the symbol can remain **TM** or be changed to **®** Trademarks are used to identify products and to distinguish them from competitors' products.

There are three general types of trademarks, and all three can apply to your new product:
1. **Word Mark** – usually a brand name.
   (i.e. Mercedes-Benz, SUNOCO)
2. **Design Mark** – or logo.
   (i.e. Bayer cross, the Mercedes-Benz three-point star)
3. **Trade Dress** – the shape and colour of a tablet or capsule; the shape, configuration and colour of a dispensing device.
   (i.e. Coca-Cola bottle)

Customers will identify a product by factors such as its name, colour, shape and size, and these trademarks are perceived as an indication of quality. Marketing management should be involved in the selection of trademarks for the product, and the trademarks should be registered with the Canadian Intellectual Property Office.

Registration of a trademark gives the manufacturer an exclusive right to use the trademark across Canada. The application process often takes a year or more, thus it is important to file it at this stage in the process.

The Canadian Intellectual Property office has an excellent guide to help you understand trademark selection and use. It can be accessed at: **http://strategis.ic.gc.ca/sc_mrksv/cipo/tm/tmar2000.pdf.**

Author's Launch Insights

Your communications team must follow your trademark guidelines or you risk weakening your trademark. In one organization I served, prior marketers failed to use trademark notations, which led to competitors using a similar trademark claim. As a result, the strength of our claim was weakened due to a lack of diligent TM symbol use, though we had filed for a registered trademark. Maintaining our trademark would have afforded a competitive difference in the market place, yet we lost this due to carelessness in our advertising and promotional materials. Always reference your trademark, especially prior to receiving your final registered trademark.

Task 8: Establish Key Launch Milestones

Responsibility for Decision: Functional Area Leaders and Launch Team
Output: Specific, achievable and measurable milestones for launch success.

Planning Recommendations:

Establish challenging goals at the senior level and link results to individual and team performance reviews. The commitment to achieving key milestones for the brand is crucial, as they are recommended by the cross-functional launch team with the functional leads' and general manager's final approval. Because many of these milestones are stretch goals, they will need support and alignment from the senior management team.

Examples of launch milestones are:

- Regulatory target dates: prepare NDS file for submission, hold pre-submission meeting with TPD and achieve NOC within X days of receipt of mandate.
- Developing the market: X% of KOLs trained with speaker program prior to NOC.
- Medical Science Liaison team: trained and deployed within X months pre-NOC.
- Phase IV clinical trial program launched at NOC.
- Sales force allocated by X (date) pre-NOC and trained by NOC.
- Trade product available to ship to pharmacies X days after NOC.
- Sample product available to ship to sales representatives within X days of NOC.
- Gain market access in targeted provinces: ON, AL, BC and PQ within X days of launch.

Author's Launch Insights

To prepare for the launch of a gastrointestinal drug, the leadership team established aggressive milestones for launch. One milestone was to launch the drug within days of NOC. This goal was surpassed and the company launched the drug one day post-NOC as a result of teamwork focused on a common goal.

Task 9:
Common Drug Review Consultation

Responsibility for Decision: Market Access
Output: Gain opinion from Common Drug Review (CDR) regarding data gaps in the economic value message of the brand.

Planning Recommendations:

CDR consultations commence early in the process to identify data gaps in the formulary listing process, and they greatly impact decisions on provincial formulary listings and subsequent market access. Realistically, time will not likely permit new trials within a meaningful timeframe to suit the CDR submission, but new analysis of existing data and re-analysis or re-packaging of possible economic messages will still be possible.

Background

The Common Drug Review at the Canadian Agency for Drugs and Technologies in Health (CADTH) is a pan-Canadian process for conducting objective, rigorous reviews of a drug's cost-effectiveness and clinical and patient evidence. CDR also provides formulary listing recommendations to Canada's publicly funded drug plans (except in Quebec).

For more information, please refer to the CADTH website: **www.cadth.ca/en/products/cdr/cdr-overview**.

Task 10: Develop & Initiate Market Research Plan

Responsibility for Decision: Market Research
Output: Obtain a 360-degree view of the market opportunity.

Planning Recommendations:

Complete a comprehensive, competitive review of the market including:
- Secondary prescription and sales market analysis (IMS CompuScript, CDH and Brogan data).

- Prescriptions by specialty group (to determine which specialists, if any, play an active role in the market).
- Current treatment algorithms by indication.
- Current reimbursement landscape, which may include competitive pricing and distribution method, public/ private reimbursement split by target indication, competitive reimbursement status and hospital formulary status, if applicable.
- Competitive intelligence on key competitors including patent and promotion information and, if possible, on future competitors.
- Review and selection of best analogues for forecasting purposes.
- Preliminary qualitative opportunity assessment research with prescribers (small sample of relevant specialties) and KOLs.

This complete review will help to:
- Identify trends in customer attitudes and behaviours in the market.
- Document perceived strengths and weaknesses of existing products and therapies.
- Identify existing unmet and emerging needs in the market (patient, physician, pharmacist and payor).
- Obtain customer reaction to preliminary product concept.

It is imperative that market research is conducted at the right time in order to provide the greatest value to the product's development.

Author's Launch Insights

I suggest a unique approach to ensure that the commercial team understands the importance of market research planning. Ask your market analytics team to provide an overview of the stages of market research to the launch team based on the product's needs at various stages of development. In addition to other benefits, this eliminates redundancies in spending.

Task 11:
Detailed Initial Commercial Assessment

Responsibility for Decision: NPP and Launch Team
Output: A thorough commercial opportunity assessment and ranking of brand priority.

Planning Recommendations:

Prior to determining a launch "Go" or "No Go" decision while in Strategic Decision Point 1, the NPP and launch team must complete an initial, yet comprehensive, assessment of the brand's potential, which characterizes the launch in terms of size, critical issues and whether it is a general practice or specialist opportunity.

Author's Launch Insights

I strongly recommend developing at least your commercial assessment and five-year strategic plan as prose documents, rather than using a haphazard Microsoft PowerPoint. PowerPoint plans do not capture adequate background for future reference. The value in a prose document comes from the detailed background on decision-making that may be useful later. As we all know well, staff turns over quickly in many organizations due to promotions and other opportunities. A detailed document will allow beliefs and assumptions to be recorded. If time and resources are an issue, hire a strategic planning consultant to support this valuable activity.

Task 12:
Corporate-Wide Launch Awareness

Responsibility for Decision: NPL Team and Corporate Communications

Output: Create awareness of the new product and the type of patient treated.

Planning Recommendations:

Once Strategic Decision Point 1 is completed, the team will need to partner with internal Corporate Communications to develop the right internal messaging. To build enthusiasm, a corporate kick-off meeting can be an important initiative. It will create awareness and excitement about the new product opportunity and help to generate support over the next twenty-one months leading up to the launch.

Author's Launch Insights

For each launch, I offered what I called "product launch town hall meetings" for ease of communication within an organization. These meetings are an opportunity to introduce your product to the entire company and gain support for improved patient care. Holding these meetings on a regular basis builds support and enthusiasm, and tracks product progress too. They are also an opportunity to give your launch team positive exposure in front of the rest of the organization for members' professional development.

Task 13:
Pricing Strategy: Pricing, Market Access Plan, Confirm Global Price Strategy & Price Corridor

Responsibility for Decision: Market Access
Output: Hold meetings with PMPRB to determine comparators and price tests, and to book meetings with CDR and provincial payors regarding pricing strategy to maximize market access and value.

Planning Recommendations:

Make market access a priority, because it is likely the most important variable in a product's lifecycle, from its development to the negotiation of an exclusive tendered contract post-genericization.

An important consideration in this area is the global price strategy. We no longer have the freedom we had in the past with a global product launch. Price restrictions, including reference pricing, profit limitations, and price reductions have created a global market with increasing price constraints. Launching in one country may have immediate ramifications in other countries, and pricing decisions can impact other markets despite the best efforts of the company. In this increasingly complex global marketplace, companies must use segmentation analysis, clinical and health outcomes research, parallel trade evaluation, political, economic, social and technological (PEST) analysis, and demand analysis to create a coordinated global pricing strategy that will anticipate regulatory challenges. While extremely difficult to create, an effective, comprehensive global launch strategy more than justifies the costs.

SUMMARY OF STRATEGIC DECISION POINT 1

One of the first steps in launching a product is determining the product's priority within the company. This is based on the value of potential sales for the product and the investment required for a successful launch. The detailed commercial assessment completed at this stage provides the organization with the required information to make "Go" or "No-Go" decisions in the marketplace. If a product appears to be a "No-Go, the following questions must be asked: What can be done to make it a "Go"? What plan is required to reach that goal? Considerable resources are invested in the research and development, or acquisition of a licensed product, and the launch team must find a way to successfully market this product.

To complete Strategic Decision Point 1, the following steps must be completed:

- Product has been formally transferred to New Product Planning (NPP).
- New Product Launch (NPL) team leader and team are chosen and are meeting routinely.
- Brand project codes and a preliminary expense budget are set.
- Guidance on the New Drug Submission (NDS) is received and the product monograph is written.
- Canadian patents and trademarks are established.
- Detailed initial commercial assessment is completed.
- A forecast and profit and loss (P&L) assessment has been done
- Established launch goals and metrics are outlined.

With these milestones reached, the NPL team is at Strategic Decision Point 1. Now, the team, with senior management, will assess:

- Go/Kill: What is required to make the brand a "Go"?
- Brand priority recommendations: A/B/C
- Key brand issues

An outright kill is unlikely at this stage, given an initial "go" decision at 24 months prior to launch. Yet, key issues will remain and should be honestly addressed, such as gaps in the product profile that require additional studies or analysis. Brand prioritization should be assessed by the team to help the organization order its workload.

Parameters for recommendation include:
- Size of the market opportunity.
- Compound attractiveness: including cost-effectiveness (price/reimbursement).
- Risk and probability of success.
- Forecasted costs and return on investment.
- Therapeutic fit within corporate priorities, such as primary care or specialty specifications.

With the elements of Strategic Decision Point 1: Developing the Company addressed and all tasks initiated, the NPL team is prepared to move onto **Strategic Decision Point 2: Developing the Product.**

Author's Launch Insights

As you develop communication tools, keep in-mind the time required for French translation. A dosage card may take a few days for translation from English to French, yet a product monograph may require as long as 6 weeks to translate. Build translation time lines into your planning horizon.

DEVELOP THE PRODUCT

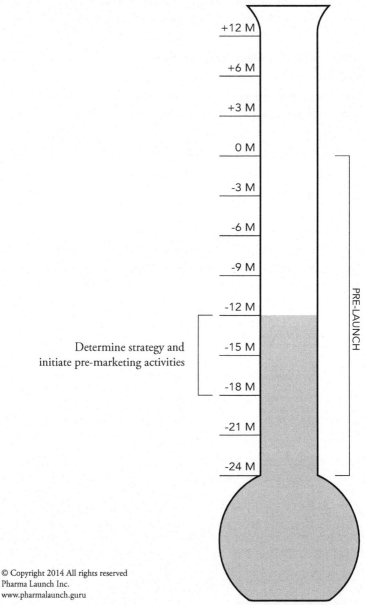

+12 M

+6 M

+3 M

0 M

-3 M

-6 M

-9 M

-12 M

Determine strategy and
initiate pre-marketing activities

-15 M

-18 M

-21 M

-24 M

PRE-LAUNCH

STRATEGIC DECISION POINT 2: DEVELOP THE PRODUCT

The key questions to answer at Strategic Decision Point 2 are:
1. How can we best capitalize on the market opportunity?
2. What does excellence look like for this opportunity?

Tasks Initiated at Twenty Months Pre-Launch

The second strategic decision point within the launch process focuses on developing the product and its overarching launch. It is executed by establishing the necessary strategies within the prelaunch and launch plan.

Based on the commercial assessment completed in the earlier stage, key insights into the market must be validated through market research before finalizing the brand strategy. Brand positioning and product pricing must also be considered. The detailed commercial assessment has already provided the information to make the "Go" or "No-Go" decision.

The brand strategy provides a sense of how the company will focus on achieving the potential of the product. At this strategic decision point, the team completes a launch plan that includes key issues, strategic imperatives and goals. The launch plan will clearly define competitors, patient and physician profiles, other targeted health care professionals, stakeholders, brand positioning, key goals, assumptions, metrics comprising sales, market share and required investments, as well as the strategies to guide how these goals will be achieved.

The following section provides milestones for the development of the product to achieve launch excellence. The following table lists the steps, along with the responsible team leads and the time to begin execution of each task.

Table 4: Summary of tasks starting at twenty months pre-launch

Item	Task	Lead	Completion
1	Develop KOL Mapping and KOL Strategy	NPP	L–20 months
2	Consult with PMPRB Experts	Market Access	L–20 months
3	Prepare Strategic Brand Plan	NPP	L–20 months
4	Prepare Pricing Strategy	Market Access	L–18 months
5	Perform Market Research	Market Research	L–18 months
6	Branding	NPP	L–18 months
7	Forecasting	NPP	L–18 months
8	Key Assumptions	NPP	L–15 months
9	Launch Planning	Marketing	L–15 months
10	Life Cycle Management (LCM) Planning	NPP	L–15 months
11	Initiation of Pre-launch Activities with KOLs and Advocates	NPP	L–12 months
12	Certificate of a Pharmaceutical Product (CPP)	Regulatory	L–12 months
13	Customer Segmentation and Customer Targeting	Sales Effectiveness	L–12 months
14	File New Drug Submission	Regulatory	L–12 months
15	LASA Assessment	Regulatory	L–12 months
16	Selection of Agency of Record (AOR)	Marketing	L–12 months
17	Transfer Product to In-line Product Management	Marketing	L–12 months
18	Launch Timing Confirmation	Regulatory	L–12 months
19	Production and Packaging Components	Supply	L–12 months

20	Packaging Development	Supply	L–12 months
21	Sales Force Planning	Sales Effectiveness	L–12 months
22	Product Training	Training	L–12 months
23	Commence Tactical Plan	Marketing	L–12 months
24	Deploy MSLs	Medical	L–12 months
25	Product P&L Update	Financial Partners/ Marketing	L–12 months
26	Special Access Program	Market Access / Regulatory	L–12 months

Task 1:
Develop Key Opinion Leader (KOL) Mapping & Strategy

Responsibility for Decision: NPP, CHE Manager, Medical and Marketing
Output: Key Opinion Leader (KOL) strategy and KOL database

Planning Recommendations

Establish a long-term KOL strategy and identify the most suitable KOLs for advisory and educational roles.

Consider the following while establishing your KOL plan: investigators who have had the opportunity to gain hands-on experience with the product are potential expert advocates as they communicate product results and experiences through publications, presentations at scientific meetings and acting as expert advisors for TPD. The next section provides additional KOL selection criteria.

Key Opinion Leaders (KOL)

All pharmaceutical companies actively engage key opinion leaders in their drug development process. Key opinion leaders are physicians who are held in high esteem by their peers. Their inputs can be invaluable while conducting clinical trials. Since they are experts in their fields, they also have the ability to influence their peers' medical practices and prescribing behaviours. Identification and development of lasting relationships with thought leaders builds an invaluable network of advocates to facilitate communication plans. It also provides feedback on messaging, tactics and product positioning.

KOL Development

A key step in developing a KOL strategy is to identify the right KOLs for the company's advisory boards through criteria based on marketing and medical objectives. Once identified, KOLs can be separated using primary and secondary research methods to create custom lists of KOLs. KOL attributes include: publication activity, clinical trial history, affiliations, committee memberships, willingness to advocate with government and payors for patient benefit and event (attendance) history. Excellent agencies with tremendous experience in KOL development are available, and where budgets allow, should be utilized.

In summary, KOL development considerations are:
- KOL mapping: identify the optimal opinion leaders.
- Develop partnership contracts for all KOLs.
- Identify spokespeople and media-train the KOLs.
- Conduct advisory boards, consensus meetings and round-tables.
- Develop slide kit, CHE strategy and treatment guidelines.
- Develop KOL group in alignment with product strategy and market access strategy.
- Leverage thought leaders amongst their peers.
- Ensure involvement in KOL launch symposium development.

Author's Launch Insights

When attending global scientific meetings, invite your KOLs and the Canadian physicians to participate in a Canadian-only session. This will provide a tremendous opportunity to hear your customers' issues and opportunities before they return to Canada with their product opinions. Your customers will niche your product quickly, and you want your product positioned in the most favourable light when they return to Canada.

Educational Focus

The KOLs should be clinical specialists who have experience with the new drug through Phase III trials or who have attended an earlier physician expert workshop.

A KOL's role is to take physician groups through the scientific and clinical background, present clinical trial results and the benefits of the new product in order to field questions and address concerns among the local specialists.

Market Intelligence:
- Probe the experts for their perceptions and expectations of the new product.
- Brainstorm for the critical success factors that will enhance market entry.
- Determine prescribing intentions: Where is the new product positioned within their practice? Which products will be displaced?
- Ask for their support as potential advocates for the new product when it is launched.

KOL Advisory Board

There are two advisory board objectives to meet when preparing the product prior to launch:

1. Develop relationships with the key influential physicians who will help drive demand and influence market access for the new product.
2. Seek advice on the product's direction.

The focus of pre-launch activities must remain scientific and educational. Ideally, investigators having hands-on experience with the new product should be developed as expert advocates, spreading the word through publications and scientific presentations at meetings, as well as acting as expert advisors for TPD and working with the market access team to assist in market access plans.

Author's Launch Insights

Where possible, consult with the sales management team regarding KOL selection criteria. When the sales team understands the launch strategy and KOL selection criteria, there will be greater support for the launch of your product and a culture of collaboration will be established.

Ask yourself why you are holding KOL meetings and be absolutely certain your objectives are clear: establishing a long-term strategy for KOL development rather than holding a KOL meeting for the sake of another meeting. Develop a solid, ongoing strategy. Keep the KOL core team small. Be prepared to access the KOL team often. Talk to medical and clinical specialists to see who has had experience with your product prior to commercial development. Today, many suppliers offer online advisory board meeting services — leverage this cost-effective means of communication for meetings.

Task 2: Consult with PMPRB Experts

Responsibility for Decision: Market Access and Pricing
Output: Input on pricing strategy for product.

Planning Recommendations:

It is extremely beneficial to establish a launch pricing consultation with the Patented Medicine Pricing Review Board (PMPRB). This dialogue will allow for PMPRB's opinion regarding comparators, possible categories and pricing suggestions. Although PMPRB's opinion is not definitive at this point, this dialogue may support final pricing strategy.

Author's Launch Insights

When presenting your data to key payors, I recommend asking a KOL to attend who has experience with your product and/or the medical/regulatory person responsible for the product approval. Where the payor has questions regarding clinical decisions, your medical team is best suited to respond to queries.

Task 3: Prepare Strategic Brand Plan

Responsibility for Decision: NPP, NPL Team and In-line Marketing
Output: New Product Launch (NPL) team to develop five-year strategic plan (key elements of a strategic plan are outlined in the Appendix).

Planning Recommendations:

A strategic plan will focus on a five-year timeline and is an extension of launch planning. It requires input from all launch team members due to their experiences in relevant areas. Marketing is responsible for the majority of the strategic plan development; other key functional areas will develop specific components of the plan, including the terms of a licensed agreement, legal pertaining to patents and branding, marketing, market access, training, supply, quality assurance, regulatory, sales operations and key account plans.

Author's Launch Insights

Develop a robust strategic planning process for your organization! I recommend an annual process for the entire commercial team. Each year conduct a strategic planning kick-off with the marketing, sales leadership and market access teams. Establish consistency in definitions and the business planning format for all areas of the commercial team. Strategic planning is the most important document developed by the commercial team, so be sure to allow sufficient time for a thorough business review assessment, analysis of data and involvement of all work streams.

Task 4: Prepare Pricing Strategy

Responsibility for Decision: Market Access, NPP and Regulatory
Output: To determine comparators and price tests, and to develop pricing strategy in order to maximize market access and value.

Planning Recommendations:

Based on meetings with PMPRB, determine comparators and price tests, and then book meetings with the Common Drug Review (CDR), provincial payors and key third-party payors regarding pricing strategy during development.

Making market access a priority is paramount; it is likely the most important variable in a product's lifecycle, from a new product launch to negotiating an exclusive contract after generic entry. Vital to the success of any product is gaining a favourable price that will meet profitability targets and gain access to targeted payors.

Author's Launch Insights

With the development of the five-year strategic plan, it is recommended to involve the services of an outside consultant to offer perspective on key components within the strategic plan such as:

- *A business review/landscape review to ensure the plan is comprehensive and accurate .*
- *A SWOT (Strengths, Weaknesses, Opportunities and Threats) analysis assessment to eliminate author bias.*
- *A forecasting exercise to develop worst case, best case and most likely forecast scenarios.*

In my experience, not everyone uses the same approach to develop a SWOT, which can result in misleading and inaccurate development of key issues.

Task 5: Perform Market Research

Responsibility for Decision: Market Research and NPP
Output: Determine product positioning and potential barriers to product adoption based on market insights and positioning research.

Planning Recommendations:

Base the ideal product positioning and potential barriers on the following secondary and primary research:

1. **Secondary market research initiatives:**
   - Measure ongoing competitive intelligence of key competitors, their existing and potential activity and relevant market issues.
   - Track ongoing market trends (Rx and sales market analysis), including market size, performance, composition, competitive mix and penetration.
   - Assess regulatory, pricing and market access issues, and perform provincial formulary monitoring.
   - Establish framework for required pre-launch market development activities.
   - Develop framework for forecasting scenarios.

2. **Primary Market Research Initiatives**
   - Conduct comprehensive qualitative market research to establish preliminary positioning concepts, identify any behavioural barriers to prescribing and gain a comprehensive understanding of the market dynamics. This research should occur in several provinces and be a sample large enough to have representation from target segments.
   - Conduct comprehensive quantitative market research to understand market dynamics, usage and attitude and needs assessments. This research may include segmentation and one or more customer groups.

Author's Launch Insights

Get the positioning right before you launch! With one brand, we completed three rounds of positioning research with 150 GPs and specialists across Canada. Your message needs to resonate with your customer. Today, there are cost-effective options for early positioning research which yield accurate results.

Task 6: Branding

Responsibility for Decision: Corporate Communications, Marketing, Legal, and possibly, Global Marketing
Output: Branding guidelines including brand name, logo, imagery, and overall look and feel of brand.

Planning Recommendations:

As customer groups are influenced by U.S. media, establish consistent branding for both the Canadian and U.S. markets to leverage awareness of the brand, if possible.

The mechanical elements of the brand itself can be defined as the name and logo. Generally, branding is a much larger concept and includes other elements, such as an icon, colours, imagery and specific font and size choice, which are consistently used in communications. The process of brand creation is an important launch component, because branding helps customers identify, recognize and remember the product.

The branding also relates to the product's positioning. That position is based on:

- Target customer perceptions of competitor products.
- Perceptions of targeted customers about the product's target product profile.
- The unique and believable characteristics of the brand that will result in adoption of the brand by the broadest possible group of patients.

Once final positioning is established, the branding needs to support this positioning. For example, if the positioning is "the fastest-acting proton pump inhibitor," then the branding needs align with this concept, all the way to name selection.

Nexium® is a great example of branding. It clearly created, in its very name, the concept of being the "next" leader. It also had uplifting, supportive colours and imagery that demonstrated its superiority and speed.

Task 7: Forecasting

Responsibility for Decision: NPP and Market Research
Output: Epidemiological (patient-based) forecast and national and regional forecasts in the following formats: dollar sales, extended units and total prescriptions (TRx) based on share of market.

Planning Recommendations:

Develop each forecast based on key learning points from market research, market access timing and KOL input. As the launch gets closer, the sophistication of forecasts increases as the marketer gains more experience with the market.

Forecasters should follow a consistent process that instills confidence in the management team. Stronger forecasts can be created by building multiple forecast models from the ground up. The most appropriate method for the development of a reliable forecast is to use analogs that represent similar product growth trends. Multiple forecasts are recommended, including all trade and sample SKUs. Many marketing consultants, are capable of developing good, reliable forecasts based on market analogs.

Types of forecasts required at the different strategic stages of launch development:

- **Develop the Company: Strategic Decision Point 1** – patient or epidemiological model (no sampling) and national five-to-ten-year dollars and units.

- **Develop the Product: Strategic Decision Point 2** – demand models will include forecast dollar and unit sales by SKU for year one and year two on a regional basis and will include sample format units.

- **Develop the Market: Strategic Decision Point 3** – fill product launch pipeline by forecasting the channel load for launch by wholesaler, retail chain and hospital, and by establishing pull-through sales targets for sales team compensation.

Author's Launch Insights

Proper forecasting relies on methods and tools that bring rigour to the process. It is essential to avoid oversimplification, which can create forecasts that ignore business cycles and seasonality, which then leads to missed expectations or excess inventory. One additional word of caution: minimize oversupply of a new product. New products typically have shorter dating within the first year of launch, due to the quality assurance stability data being new. As a result, shelf life is usually shorter on new products for both samples and trade SKUs. Be careful to not be overly positive in your forecasting, to avoid costly write-offs and returns from expired product. Another suggestion to enhance forecasting and reduce long-term costs is to develop a company-wide analog library based on a variety of launches and launch variables.

Task 8: Key Assumptions

Responsibility for Decision: NPP and Cross-functional Team
Output: Identify all key planning assumptions for all functional areas as a basis for planning.

Planning Recommendations:

Update key assumptions regularly. In strategic planning, an assumption is an assertion about a characteristic of the future, either a market event or an internal corporate-driven event, which underlies the current operations or plans of an organization.

Examples of key assumptions based on market events:
- Product XYZ is at risk of Notice of Allegation (NOA) in June 2015.
- Forecasted dollar value of the authorized generic is based on 25% of brand price.
- Two new product entries will increase market growth rate to 12%.

Table 5: Key brand assumptions

Key Area	2015 Key Brand Assumptions (for either in-line or new products)
Product	• Product XYZ Average Rx value in 2015: $49.52 • Rx length in Quebec: 23.5 days • Average Rx length in ROC: 57.3 days • Average SKU split: 10 mg, 9%; 15 mg, 25%; 20 mg, 46% and 30 mg, 20% • Ex-factory pull-through ratio: 112% • No patent risks to product during 2015
Market	• Drug class market expected to grow at 9.8% in 2015
Competition	• There will be three direct competitors promoting their products

Customer (at 100% achievement of targeted sales)	• Total details: 60,086 calls • First detail: 45,345 calls • Second detail: 12,342 calls • Third detail: 2,399 calls • Targeted customer groups: Cardiologist (D1–D6) • Primary Care Physicians (D1–D5) • 2015 A&P Spend: $453 K (including samples at $987 K)

Task 9: Launch Planning

Responsibility for Decision: NPP, NPL Team and Marketing
Output: Pre-launch tactics for execution preceding launch and launch plan tactics.

Planning Recommendations:

Once the five-year strategic plan is approved, the launch plan should be completed in two stages: pre-launch tactics and post-launch tactics. The intent is to have a strategy in place first, then begin executing pre-launch tactics that support this strategy while finalizing the launch plan. Although the launch plan will be discussed in an upcoming section of this document, note that the current strategic plan and pre-launch plan are the most significant pieces of the overall launch plan, which will include a final portion of post-launch tactics as well.

Together, the pre-launch plan and post-launch tactics, along with the five- year strategic plan comprise the new product plan. Marketing is responsible for the majority of the launch plan development; members of other key functional areas will also develop its components. A pre-launch plan outline is given in the Appendix and offers a guideline to effective launch planning based on established marketing principles.

With the ongoing growth of social media, it may be considered as a tactic. However, social media has limitations due to promotional guidelines established by the Pharmaceutical Advertising Advisory Board (PAAB) and Advertising Standards Canada (ASC). Where possible, social media offers awareness of new products and provides greater insight into customer needs.

Task 10:
Life Cycle Management (LCM) Planning

Responsibility for Decision: NPP and Cross-functional Team
Output: Establish a product LCM plan and gain approval for LCM strategies and budgets.

Planning Recommendations:

This task is essential in order to increase the profitability of product throughout the product lifecycle.

Establish a timeframe and objectives for product lifecycle management development activities.

Task 11:
Initiation of Pre-launch Activities with KOLs & Advocates

Responsibility for Decision: NPP, Medical and Regulatory
Output: Building awareness with key customers and targeted specialists.

Planning Recommendations:

Focus efforts through KOL development and market research to build awareness and advocacy for the new product.

Now is the time to set the stage for the new product launch. Pre-launch awareness and interest can be extremely well developed using enabling activities that are subtle, yet influential. The main objective of this pre-launch activity is to develop key influential clinicians who will drive demand for the product. Scientific and educational enabling activities will include communicating through publications, presentations at scientific meetings and building a team of advocates, all of which will escalate throughout the registration period.

Once the NDS has been accepted for review, stronger assumptions about the product profile, indications, dosage and competitive claims for the product can be made. At this point, the market situation should be reviewed and an action plan established to ensure a successful launch. The business review forms the building blocks for the pre-launch marketing plan. The goal of any product launch is to deliver a unique and superior product: a differentiated product that brings new benefits and added value to customers.

Here are a few considerations about your new product in development:

1. Is the product truly an innovative and novel product offering, or is it simply a "me too" type of drug?
2. What are the product's unique benefits relative to those of competitors?
3. Does the product solve customers' problems relative to their needs?
4. Does the product meet unfulfilled customer needs better than competitors' products can?

At this point, there are three key programs to consider as part of an impactful market development program:
1.   Clinical trial publication plans.
2.   Communication efforts with medical science liaisons.
3.   Clinical experience programs, such as Phase III and IV clinical trials.

Clinical Trial Publication Plan

An effective method to create awareness within the medical community is through published articles and study reports in medical journals. During the market development stage when the NDS is under review, published clinical trials are quite effective at raising awareness and creating interest in the product. Consider Pre-clinical, Phase II and Phase III studies for publication as well.

Drafting manuscripts for publication can be completed by clinical investigators or by using a medical copywriter's services to prepare a manuscript under the lead author's guidance. All manuscripts must be reviewed and edited by a medical copywriter prior to submission to journals.

When considering where to publish, consider the target market for the new product and choose the journals most appropriate to attract that market. Publication in respected peer-reviewed journals is the preferred outcome. Consider publication in Canadian medical association journals to increase awareness amongst the target market. Many Canadian clinical trials have been published in highly respected journals such as The New England Journal of Medicine, The British Medical Journal and The Lancet. The more prestigious the journal, the more influence publication will have on the targeted medical audience.

Some new products are truly innovative and offer significant improvements in treatments, while others offer less substantial improvements. Where clinical findings are significant, there is a higher probability of publishing the clinical trial results in a well-respected international journal.

Phase IIIB and IV Clinical Trial Programs

Use of a clinical trial program is an ideal approach to building experience amongst key clinicians. Provide an opportunity for specialists to experience the product with their patient population and involve them directly in the development of the product at an early stage.

The creation of clinical trials is based on the lifecycle management program completed during the product's development stage. Clinical trial alignment considerations include: enhancing market access, gaining key opinion leader support, establishing competitive comparisons, new dosages, expanding the market through new indications and entering potentially new or existing patient populations.

Another key component of the clinical trial program is to include influential clinicians as subject matter experts and advisors to help design and implement new clinical trials. During earlier phase trials, a small, yet select group of clinical specialists was involved in the product development. At this point, clinical trials can involve a larger number of specialists in targeted geographical areas to plan and execute Phase IIIB and Phase IV trials.

Compiling a database of specialists based on their key areas of influence and their capabilities to conduct clinical trials will guide the medical team and medical science liaisons to recruit appropriate clinicians to design protocols aligned with launch activities.

This is an ideal time, based on the product's life cycle management strategic plan, to design future clinical trials and to maintain high levels of interest amongst influential clinicians. It is best to commence key clinical trials just after receiving the NOC. The following section highlights the differences between Phase IIIB and Phase IV trials.

Phase IIIB Trials:
- Have investments pertaining to the life cycle management program.
- Require Clinical Trial Applications (CTA) with TPD, subject to Ethics Review Board approval processes.
- May commence prior to NOC; a recommendation is to delay the start of the trial to allow the NDS review process to remain focused on existing data.
- May focus on areas outside the approved indication for the product.
- Used to expand the scope of the current indication for wider patient group targets or for pursuing other therapeutic areas.
- May focus on new formulations or delivery systems to improve the product profile or gain extended patent protection.

Phase IV Trials:
- Are considered post-marketing studies and commence after a new product is granted NOC.
- Require Clinical Trial Applications (CTA) with TPD, subject to Ethics Review Board approval processes.
- Offer an opportunity to extend the clinical experience to key clinicians who were not involved in earlier trial programs.
- Are ideal for developing pharmacoeconomics or cost-benefit data; a recommendation is to involve an epidemiologist in the development of the pharmacoeconomics protocol.
- Use key competitors for comparisons with study reports designed for review by formulary groups.
- Investigate and partner with formulary committees to understand their needs and experiences with other products.

Task 12:
Certificate of a Pharmaceutical Product (CPP)

Responsibility for Decision: Regulatory
Output: A CPP or good manufacturing practices (GMP)
certificate for one year.

Planning Recommendations:

There are differences with the approval process for a CPP when a drug is manufactured in Canada as opposed to a drug manufactured by a foreign company. For detailed information on the different requirements, visit the Health Canada website.

Task 13:
Customer Segmentation & Customer Targeting

Responsibility for Decision: Sales Effectiveness and NPP
Output: Identify key prescriber targets and preliminary sales force deployment, which affects targeting and financial assumptions.

Planning Recommendations:

Once the NDS has passed the initial screening period and the review process is on track, it is time to begin developing a strong KOL support base for the launch. In addition, segmentation of all targeted customers will assist in determining the promotional priority and size of the product's sales team.

Task 14: File New Drug Submission

Responsibility for Decision: Regulatory
Output: Earliest possible date of submission to TPD for NDS or SNDS (supplemental new drug submission).

Planning Recommendations:

Upon acceptance for review, provide relevant sections of submission to market access.

Task 15:
Look Alike Sound Alike (LASA) Assessment

Responsibility for Decision: Regulatory
Output: Conduct an assessment to ensure look-alike and sound-alike attributes are not likely to cause confusion with another health product approved by Health Canada.

Planning recommendations:

A brand name LASA assessment is required for all submissions types for biologics and pharmaceutical prescription drugs where a brand name is being proposed or a change to an existing brand name is proposed. Failure to provide a LASA assessment may result in not receiving a DIN/NOC.

Task 16:
Selection of Agency of Record (AOR)

Responsibility for Decision: Marketing
Output: Establish Agency of Record (AOR) for the brand.

Planning Recommendations:

Select the AOR early so that the launch team will invite a higher level of input from the agency, thus leveraging its launch experience.

Task 17:
Transfer Product to In-line Product Management

Responsibility for Decision: NPP and In-line Marketing
Output: Product is transitioned to in-line marketing for future strategic planning and tactical implementation of the launch plan.

Planning Recommendations:

The transfer of product responsibility to the in-line marketing team needs to occur approximately twelve months prior to receiving the Notice of Compliance (NOC).

The rationale for the timing of this transfer to the in-line marketing team is as follows:

- It affords opportunities for the marketing team to develop KOL relationships early in the product's lifecycle via advisory boards, symposia, congresses, etc.
- It develops stronger brand knowledge among the in-line marketers, who are the future brand advocates.
- This transition expedites the learning curve for the marketers well in advance of launch.
- It develops a product expert for the sales training team prior to NOC.
- It establishes ownership of the product prior to launch.

Task 18: Launch Timing Confirmation

Responsibility for Decision: Regulatory
Output: Estimate NOC target date based on file status at TPD.

Planning Recommendations:

Calculate the earliest possible new product approval, and then determine the probability of outcome for all targeted dates. The TPD suggests that the earliest possible approval target is a 345-day review for new product submission.

Author's Launch Insights

Build all launch plans based on NOC timing.
Caveat: launch too early and you will not be prepared.
Caveat: launch too late and you will have competitive issues, because timing into market will affect maximum sales uptake; order of entry can affect your brand's outcome. If you are tenth to market in a class of drugs and offer no substantial benefit over other drugs, your uptake will be limited, while if your drug is novel, the chances of higher uptake and favourable pricing will be different.

Task 19: Production and Packaging Components

Responsibility for Decision: Supply and Quality Assurance (QA)
Output: Production and packaging status report, launch quantities, product samples, retail stocking and distribution plans.

Planning Recommendations:

Ensure launch quantities and product availability is on track based on launch milestones.

Task 20: Packaging Development

Responsibility for Decision: Supply and NPL Team
Output: Status report on production and packaging, including product and packaging availability and timing, along with forecasted launch quantities.

Planning Recommendations:

Conduct primary market research with patients, pharmacists and wholesalers to assess best packaging options.

- Will the packaging artwork be developed, approved and ready with lot number and expiry date to meet the launch date?
- To minimize any delays between NOC and stock shipments, can labels be printed in advance and overprinted with the Drug Identification Numbers (DINs)?
- Are all packaging components available?
- Will the packaging be completed and awaiting label application?
- Are there any QA issues to be resolved prior to launch?

Developing Dress Package

It cannot be stressed enough that a critical factor in any launch is the presentation of the product. It is always difficult to anticipate launch demand, but it is crucial to build a demand model to reflect the anticipated monthly uptake over the first two to three years post-launch.

Key packaging components for approval are:
1. Shipper.
2. Carton.
3. Bottle/delivery system.
4. Package insert.
5. Packaging design.
6. Approval of label copy.
7. Approval of label artwork.

During the Customer Needs Analysis, preliminary concepts need to be presented for customer reaction and validation. Key considerations in determining the product presentation are:

- **Branding** – trade name, trademark and trade dress.
- **Packaging** – design, ease of use and customer preference.
- **Bilingual packaging** – format, design and artwork should be initiated.
- **Competitive product presentations** – what is the current standard of therapy? Can it be improved?
- **Market gaps** – those that may have emerged during research.
- **UPC requested** – if applicable.
- A recent **Bar Code system** is now in effect for Canadian pharmaceuticals, based on the GS1 global automated identification standard.

Further important considerations are as follows:
1. Will the product be imported in the finished format? If so, ensure that the packaging and label copy meets the specifications set out in the NDS.
2. If the product is imported in bulk and packaged in Canada, the packaging and label copy needs to comply with NDS specifications.
3. Label layout should be drafted based on expected labelling, revised if necessary when final labelling is known (two weeks prior to NOC) and finalized when the DINs are granted (five days before NOC).

4. If there are different strengths to be commercialized, ensure that the packaging easily differentiates the strengths from one another.

Author's Launch Insights

Where urgency to the market is a key consideration – as it should be in a twenty-year patent market environment – consider that once the DIN is granted, white stock could be produced. This can occur weeks before a launch to ensure pipeline fill for warehouses and targeted pharmacies. One risk of this scenario is a late NOC and the need to write off white-labeled product. The decision to produce before final approval depends on strategy and urgency to market.

Involve the supply team early as non-standard packaging, i.e. blister packs may require special packaging equipment lead time. In some cases it may even require more than a year to design, build and install.

Task 21: Sales Force Planning

Responsibility for Decision: Sales Force Effectiveness, Sales and NPP
Output: Sales force optimization plan.

Planning Recommendations:

A well-trained and sufficiently staffed field force is key to a successful launch. Prior to launch, there should also be a significant field presence to manage pre-launch KOL education and relationship development.

Here are several questions that must be answered:

1. What sales force resources are needed to make the product successful and to achieve its goals?
2. What are the existing field force capabilities with respect to the new product?
3. Is the pre-launch target audience new to the field team?
4. How much effort can the existing field team exert on the new product pre-launch activities?
5. If there is a new target audience, how many additional calls will be necessary?
6. Are the field representatives already performing to full capacity?
7. How many targeted customers need to be reached? Is there a capacity within the existing sales force to reach these customers and provide an effective call frequency?
8. Is it realistic to add this new product to the force's schedule?
9. Does the new product complement the sales force's current in-line product portfolio, or will it require the team to take an entirely new direction?
10. Which brands currently being promoted will be affected by this new brand (for example, do they fall to a lower position in the promotional mix)?

If the answers to the above questions indicate a need for increased sales presence, then sales force allocation should be identified as a key issue and must be made a strategic priority.

Author's Launch Insights

The reality of selling today is less physician access and shorter call length. The reality of selling 3–4 products on every call is simply not practical. Other promotional efforts are required, including sales pulsing, contract sales teams, and non-rep promotion. An emerging opportunity is the growth of electronic medical records as a method to increase awareness of a product.

Task 22: Product Training

Responsibility for Decision: Managers of Learning and Development, Sales and In-line Marketing
Output: Field force, sales managers and executive team are all trained based on their level of need.

Planning Recommendations:

Train all executives on product and key selling messages (KSMs) early during the training of the sales team prior to launch.

Author's Launch Insights

Key messaging is vital for all product promotion, and this starts at the top. One CEO who truly needed training on key messaging thought the new delivery device looked like a "kazoo," a child's musical instrument from the mid-1800's. He delivered this message to the investment community and to the employees. Meanwhile, the brand team was trying to establish a clear message that this device was vital for drug delivery, as the targeted disease was life-threatening. Obviously, all members of the team need to be aligned regarding key messages.

Task 23: Commence Tactical Plan Activities

Responsibility for Decision: In-line Marketing
Output: Tactical plans.

Planning Recommendations:

After objectives and strategies are established, determine how those goals will become a reality. This "action" part of the plan is the most important from the standpoint of the customer, who will not see the internal planning process, read the positioning statement or know the strategies. They will, however, see and experience the activities introduced for their benefit.

Tactical activities must convey messages successfully. They should stimulate the customer to try the product and to ideally adopt the product as part of their clinical practices. Tactical plans must be written in great detail, with each program description outlining timelines and specific executable elements.

Tactical programs are developed and implemented in three different ways:
1. Tactics developed by marketing and implemented by marketing.
2. Tactics developed by marketing and implemented regionally by the sales force.
3. Tactics developed by sales and implemented regionally by the sales force.

All launch tactics must align with a key issue and strategy and provide a positive return on investment (ROI).

The launch team must present the tactical plan and highlight how it addresses each strategic issue and imperative. For example, if market access in Ontario, Quebec and British Columbia is a strategic imperative, then the tactics for pre-launch and post-launch are designed to address this imperative.

Some examples of "classic" launch tactics include the following:

KOL Symposia

During the market development stage, relationships are developed with the clinical research investigators and thought leaders involved with the product. For the most part, these customers are looking forward to the launch as much as the internal launch team. A KOL symposium is an opportunity to bring in advocates and regional opinion leaders to share their clinical experiences and to encourage their colleagues to become regional advocates for the product. The influence cascade is top-down with this approach to market development, and many product launches achieve great success with specialist endorsements. A typical KOL launch symposium includes scientific learning, case study workshops and social activities.

Continuing Health Education (CHE)

CHE provides quality medical education to enhance the understanding of best practice guidelines and latest clinical evidence for healthcare professionals. In turn, this information benefits the clinician's patients. Healthcare providers need to enhance their skills on a continual basis to benefit their patients. CHE programs are developed for a targeted healthcare provider audience. Accreditation of a CHE program should be pursued to increase provider participation and to ensure the program offers a balanced educational approach.

Peer Influencers

As the launch approaches, it is essential to expand the circle of knowledgeable clinicians by introducing the science behind the new product to local and regional specialists. An ideal venue for this purpose is an Expert Workshop, a small, informal and highly interactive forum for product introductions that is primarily educational. These peer workshops include current methodologies in disease management and new directions for therapy, and they include new and developing products. In this setting, it is important to avoid bias, to maintain the credibility of both the workshop leaders and the company.

Patient Advocacy

Patient advocacy focuses on patient education about the use of health plans and how to obtain needed care. Patient advocates include government consumer advocacy agencies that provide services to the public at large, as well as private sector for-profit and non-profit service providers.

Patient advocacy can include groups that develop policies and legislation to improve systems for patients, such as the Alzheimer's Association. Advocacy organizations are usually non-profit, focus on one disease, participate in fundraising and awareness campaigns, and run healthcare information services. These organizations normally do not engage in the provision of clinical support, nor do they act as liaisons between patient and provider.

Suggested approaches to support patient advocacy groups:
- Partnering to gain greater market access coverage and to raise disease awareness or prevention programs.
- Providing funding to support the group's day-to-day operations.
- Donating to help patient groups conduct a specific event or activity, e.g. a breast cancer awareness day.
- Educational support.

It is recommended to develop a written agreement with the advocacy group to outline the specifics of how company resources may be allocated.

Public Relations

Another way to increase awareness with both professional and consumer audiences is to develop a professional public relations campaign. Public relations (PR) is ideally introduced shortly after launch to gain the broadest media coverage, but planning for it should begin in this stage. This tactic requires a clear understanding of the target audience and relevant messages.

The best way to ensure an agency understands your strategy is to develop a detailed briefing document, which will include clear brand direction and a sound understanding of your target. See the Appendix for more information.

Media Training

When considering a public relations program, training medical spokespeople across Canada is recommended. At a minimum, develop regional spokespeople in Ontario, Quebec, West and Atlantic Canada. A PR program will likely garner national story pick-up. With trained spokespeople across the country, there will be a timely response to the media's inquiries. When selecting a PR agency, its capabilities must include media training for the physicians who will be your spokespeople. Effectively dealing with the media's inquiries will have a very positive impact. See the Appendix for more information.

Task 24:
Deploy Medical Science Liaisons (MSL)

Responsibility: Medical
Output: Establish a MSL team for communication dialogue around three key areas: scientific concepts, clinical objectives and business opportunities.

Planning Recommendation:

An MSL is a pharmaceutical or medical device company representative who communicates between the medical department of a company and the healthcare industry customers. The MSL is bound by high ethical standards and acts as an educator and company representative, utilizing his/her clinical knowledge while providing a company's product information.

MSL communications focus on three key areas: scientific concepts, clinical objectives and business opportunities. Many MSLs have an advanced scientific degree, such as an M.D. Ph.D. or Pharm.D. Essentially, MSLs provide a link between the industry and the medical community.

Furthermore, MSLs are invaluable for reducing the time to reach peak product optimization, as well as for key thought leader development and research. When considering the significant product R&D costs, the limited patent life available for pharmaceuticals and the lag to formulary approvals, companies need to rapidly increase product awareness; MSLs offer an effective, efficient method to introduce a new product without promotion to the medical community.

When deciding whether to strategically incorporate the aid of MSLs, consider the following:

1. How do MSLs fit in with the overriding launch strategy?
2. Is this a short-term or permanent strategy?
3. What is the MSL's primary focus, and how will demand for the MSL role be created or communicated?
4. What is the best timing for MSL inclusion: immediately or prior to the launch?
5. Which customers do the MSLs support: pharmacists, GP/FP, specialists?
6. To whom will the MSLs report, keeping in mind that the MSL team needs to be separate from the commercial team since its role is not to sell?
7. Is the organization structured, and does it have the capabilities, to develop the personnel hired as MSLs?
8. Which consultants, colleagues and previous companies have MSLs?
9. Out of all the functional areas, including marketing, sales, HR, medical and regulatory, what needs to be involved in the development of an MSL program?
10. What are the costs to employ a MSL?

Task 25: Product P&L update

Responsibility for Decision: Financial Partners and Marketing
Output: Updated profit and loss statement for continual assessment.

Planning recommendations:

The profit and loss (P&L) statement relies on the commercial assessment and dollar forecast, term sheet for an acquired product and key forecast assumptions relative to the supply, distribution, sales and marketing costs for the new product.

Task 26: Special Access Program (SAP)

Responsibility for Decision: Market Access and Regulatory
Output: Agreements with provinces and manufacturers to establish drug benefit prices for products reimbursed under a SAP.

Planning Recommendations:

It is important to note that the SAP is not a shortcut to the regulatory process for marketing new drugs in Canada. The program provides compassionate access to drugs on a patient-by-patient basis.

Author's Launch Insights

Another consideration prior to launch is whether to develop a company-funded patient assistance program. A specific segment of the patient population is unable to afford treatment with new, more effective drugs. Patient assistance programs respond to this need by providing free drugs to patients unable to pay for their medications. These programs can be managed via: direct distribution from the manufacturer to treating physicians, sample cards or including a small co-pay. These programs offer multiple benefits to pharmaceutical companies because patients benefit directly and positive relationships are developed between the company, physician and patient. In addition, physicians are able to gain experience with the product prior to formulary coverage.

SUMMARY OF STRATEGIC DECISION POINT 2

At the end of Strategic Decision Point 2 (now approaching launch minus six months), a significant part of the groundwork towards a successful launch has been completed as the product has been developed.

Before moving forward in the launch process, the following key initiatives should be in place:
- The NDS is filed.
- Sales force allocation plan is established.

- Launch tactical plan and budget is established.
- Regulatory dossier is completed and submitted.
- Initial five-year strategic plan including key market insights and issues established and validated through market research.
- Brand vision, strategy and positioning are established, finalized, tested and consistent with product monograph/product profile, which have been filed.
- Brand messaging is developed.
- Market access and pricing plan developed including initial value proposition.
- A preliminary price recommendation is in place.
- KOL activities, KOLs and advocates are identified and initial meetings have occurred.
- The initial LCM plan has been developed.
- Forecast and P&L assessment is updated.
- **Pre-launch plan and budget including:**
    a. KOL planning
    b. Trials
    c. MSLs
    d. Publications
    e. Public Relations
    f. Advocacy

With the above accomplished, the new product team is now prepared for **Strategic Decision Point 3**, which begins at launch minus six months. At this point, senior management will assess and confirm brand strategy, review launch metrics and goals, and approve the launch tactical plan and budget.

STRATEGIC DECISION POINT 3:
DEVELOP THE MARKET

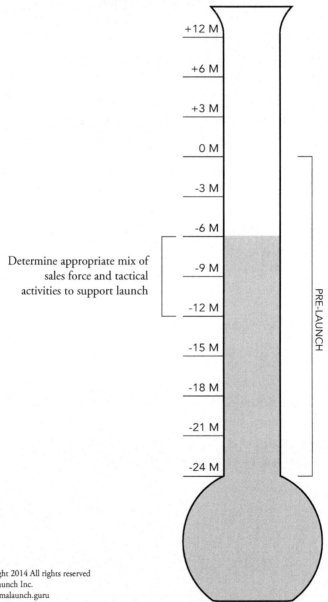

Determine appropriate mix of
sales force and tactical
activities to support launch

STRATEGIC DECISION POINT 3: DEVELOP THE MARKET

Tasks Initiated at Six Months Pre-launch

The key questions to answer at Strategic Decision Point 3 are:
1. What is the plan to maximize this opportunity?
2. What investment is needed over the next twelve months?

The next stage in the launch process is to develop the market as the team initiates pre-launch activities and ensures the NDS review is on track. It will also ensure that the NOC target date is confirmed. Other tasks will include confirmation of supply and that production planning will meet the launch target date for all volumes required.

Promotional tasks will include launch meeting planning, venue booking and promotional launch campaign development. The promotional launch will include two pieces identified for early PAAB review and all primary promotional tools being created. Pricing submissions are near completion, dialogue with payors is advancing, and the distribution plan is now finalized. Senior management can assess and confirm brand strategy, review launch metrics and goals, and approve the launch tactical plan and expenses.

The table on the following page lists the tasks to be completed in Strategic Decision Point 3: Develop the Market.

Table 6: Summary of tasks at six months pre-launch

Item	Task	Lead	Completion
1	Market Development Pre-Launch Activities	Marketing/Medical	L−6 months
2	Provincial Formulary and PMPRB Consultations	Market Access/ Regulatory	L−6 months
3	NDS Submission Update	Regulatory	L−6 months
4	Production and Packaging Components	Supply	L−6 months
5	Launch Meeting Planned	Sales Operations	L−6 months
6	Launch Plan Implementation	In-line Marketing	L−3 months
7	Financial Overview	Finance	L−6 months
8	Distribution Plan	Key Accounts	L−6 months
9	Research: Preparing to Launch	Market Research	L−6 months
10	Pricing and Reimbursement Plan	Market Access	L−6 months
11	Sales force Deployment and Training	Sales Effectiveness/ Training	L−6 months

Task 1:
Initiate Market Development Pre-Launch Activities

Responsibility for Decision: Medical and Marketing
Output: MSLs hired and trained, CHE event and public relations activities planned for execution.

Planning Recommendations:

At six months pre-launch, tactical pre-launch activities should be underway.

Task 2:
Provincial Formulary & PMPRB Consultations

Responsibility for Decision: Market Access and Regulatory Affairs
Output: Market access plans.

Planning Recommendations:

Develop advocacy connections, perform data analysis for payors, and execute trial plans to support pricing and market access needs, with these specific action steps:
- Meet with provincial drug plan managers and private payors.
- Anticipate and prepare plans for pharmacoeconomics challenges.
- Finalize submissions for public and private payors.
- Anticipate PMPRB non-excessive, average price ceiling.

Task 3:
New Drug Submission (NDS) Update

Responsibility for Decision: Regulatory
Output: NOC Status Report.

Planning Recommendations:

Review and update the file status with the estimated NOC date for the new product planning team.

Task 4:
Production and Packaging Components

Responsibility for Decision: Supply, Quality Assurance and Regulatory
Output: Determine product availability as a key component of developing the market.

Planning Recommendations:

The timing for product availability is a key consideration as the market is being developed. Review and update product manufacturing schedules and delivery timelines for both trade and product samples.

Author's Launch Insights

Focus supply production on the practical need of physician and patients. For example, where the product has multiple SKUs for titration, place priority on starting doses instead of maximum doses.

Task 5: Launch Meeting

Responsibility for Decision: Sales Operations and Sales Leadership
Output: Create overview of launch meeting plans.

Planning Recommendations:

Early planning is critical to the success of the launch meeting. Some aspects of meeting planning, such as venue selection and site inspection, should begin no less than six months prior to launch.

Here are several action steps:
- Understand rationale for launch timing: expedite launch meeting when seasonality is an issue with the product.
- Announce to internal teams the national product launch sales meeting date and venue.
- Announce to KOLs the launch meeting date and venue.
- Create meeting theme and special activities to build sales team enthusiasm.
- Develop learning objectives for meetings.
- Develop sales meeting presentation for sales leaders.
- Identify keynote speakers and chairpersons.

Author's Launch Insights

Cost effectiveness has become a key planning consideration, so combining a launch meeting with a sales meeting makes sense logistically. By adding a product launch-specific day to a sales meeting, launch costs can be reduced significantly.

Task 6: Launch Plan Implementation

Responsibility for Decision: In-line Marketing
Output: Development of launch plan tactics.

Planning Recommendations:

An early start to program implementation will improve launch success by ensuring that key programs are ready for the launch. To gain sales team buy-in, involve sales managers and representatives early in the development stage of all programs. At this time, it is necessary to validate the market environment, as well as internal partner progress.

Market Situation:
- Validate customer needs and any market gaps.
- Assess any significant competitor changes.
- Establish distribution plan with key accounts.
- Are the SWOT analysis and related assumptions still valid?
- Revisit competitive positioning status.
- Review PMPRB strategy and market access planning.
- Revisit product sales forecast: TRx and dollars.

Internal Partners:
- Supply – is the production and packaging schedule on target?
- P&L update – is expense tracking on budget?
- Marketing – write advertising agency creative briefs.
- Creative advertising – develop and test concepts.
- Marketing – develop launch symposium, advertising and mail communication programs.
- Implement KOL and primary care promotional program testing.
- Develop sales tactical programs.
- Develop patient advocacy group and KOL advocates.

Author's Launch Insights

Develop a specific set of standard programs for a launch including dosing, efficacy, safety, format and price / formulary inclusion.

Task 7: Financial Overview

Responsibility for Decision: Finance and In-line Marketing
Output: Budget forecast and updated profit and loss forecast.

Planning Recommendations:

- Validate product labelling and pricing objectives and how these changes affect unit and sales volumes.
- Is the market environment stable or in a state of flux?
- Develop an updated Advertising and Promotion (A&P) budget.
- Update the five-to-ten-year product forecast from the business review based on the current competitive environment and current labelling assumption.

Use the following information to support your forecast:
- Product price assumptions: Are there any anticipated changes?
- Competitive positioning: Are there any anticipated changes?
- Competitors at launch: Are there new entries?
- What is the updated market forecast trend?
- Life cycle assumptions: Are there additional indications or market expansion opportunities?

Identify and communicate the NOC labelling assumptions. Develop a market-based forecast model with commentary to provide rationale for the forecast.

Task 8: Distribution Plan

Responsibility for Decision: Key Accounts
Output: Key account distribution plan.

Planning Recommendations:

To further ensure a successful launch, develop a timeline of distribution deadlines for the upcoming launch in four to six months. The timeline needs to contain the details of the expected date of NOC, the launch, and the fact sheet and fax sheet for pharmacy customers.

Distribution will depend on product type: solids, liquids, special storage, specialty or general pharmacy. There are two types of distributors: wholesalers, who buy from companies and resell to pharmacies, and self-distributors, such as Shoppers Drug Mart, which buys and uses product for their own stores. In the case of products that require special storage and transportation, distribution may need to be handled by companies that are equipped to meet such needs.

Author's Launch Insights

Understanding the difference between a fill and the actual demand is key to ensure sufficient inventory at launch. Include priority customers and predict quantity for each wholesaler for an appropriate pipeline fill, remembering that pipeline fill does not equal Rx sales. The pipeline fill is greater than actual demand until a product is either discontinued or out of stock.

Task 9: Research: Preparing to Launch

Responsibility for Decision: Market Research
Output: To set the foundation for a successful launch.

Planning Recommendations:

1. Test promotional materials for impact and refine prior to printing.
2. Verify the status of the PAAB submission to ensure promotional materials are ready on time.
3. Monitor key pre-launch market development activities (CME events, conferences, etc.) for timing at launch.

4. Perform ongoing competitive intelligence on key competitors and issues in the market, including new competitors and indications.

Ongoing market trend tracking (Rx and sales market analysis) includes:
- Market size, performance, composition, competitive mix and penetration.
- Existing and potential competitive activity.
- Regulatory, pricing and market access issues, as well as provincial formulary monitoring.

Task 10: Pricing and Reimbursement Plan

Responsibility for Decision: Market Access
Output: Formulary submission and market access plans for product.

Planning Recommendations:

A drug or device's success ultimately hinges on its reimbursement profile: first line, second line, etc. It is important to include the cost parameters from the Phase III trials to optimize market access strategy. In a timely manner, prior to launch, inform all private payors of the new product.

Include pharmacoeconomics analyses where:
- The scientific validity of the trial might be jeopardized by economic components.
- The economic component cannot be customized to address regional cost issues.
- Phase III trials procedures differed from routine standards of care.
- Trial inclusion and exclusion criteria are too stringent to allow cost applications across all patient categories.

Task 11:
Sales Force Deployment and Training

Responsibility for Decision: Sales Force Effectiveness and Sales
Management
Output: Deployed and trained sales force.

Planning Recommendations:

A well-trained, sufficiently staffed field sales force is critical to the success
of a launch. Prior to launch, a significant field presence should manage
the pre-launch opinion leader education and relationship activities.
Hiring and training activities must begin well in advance of the launch
to maximize the promotional impact at launch. At this stage, the sales
force should be fully prepared.

Author's Launch Insights

*When new sales representatives are hired to sell a new product, consider hiring a
consultant to build the new representatives' physician appointment calendars. Access
is extremely limited, and establishing a productive field schedule is imperative at
launch. Companies can no longer afford to wait 3–6 months for reps to gain access
to clinicians with limited call schedules of 2–3 times or less per year. Also consider
building in lunch-and-learn, clinical rounds sponsorships, and CHE events around a
launch as part of the new sales representatives' book of appointments.*

SUMMARY OF STRATEGIC DECISION POINT 3

At the end of Strategic Decision Point 3 (now approaching launch minus three months), senior management will verify that the following key initiatives are in place:

- Assessed regulatory timing.
- Engaged in payor dialogue.
- Anticipated commercial targets, such as brand awareness levels and brand usage.
- Updated forecast: units and dollars and TRx.

The following internal launch milestones have been met:

- Product supply.
- Promotional material readiness.
- Tactical execution status versus key issues.

By the end of this stage, the launch team has developed the company, the product and the market in a manner that will ensure success through continual efforts in each of these areas. If all of the above initiatives are complete, the team is ready to proceed to **Strategic Check-in Point 4: Launch Readiness.**

STRATEGIC CHECK-IN 4:
LAUNCH READINESS

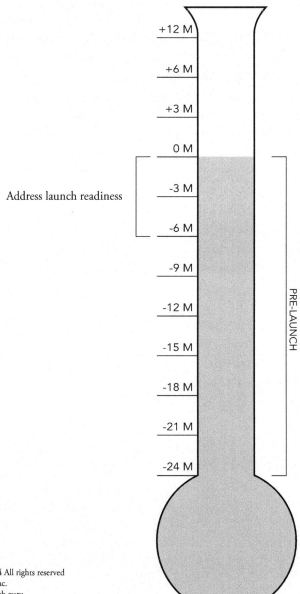

+12 M

+6 M

+3 M

0 M

Address launch readiness

-3 M

-6 M

-9 M

-12 M

-15 M

-18 M

-21 M

-24 M

PRE-LAUNCH

STRATEGIC CHECK-IN POINT 4: LAUNCH READINESS

Tasks Initiated at Three Months Pre-Launch

Key Question:
1.   Are we ready?

At this stage, the team must openly address its readiness for the pre- and post-launch process within the next six months, and identify and proactively close gaps with senior management guidance.

By Strategic Check-in Point 4, the following must be in place:
- NDS review is on track, and NOC target date is confirmed.
- Supply is secure, and production plan will meet launch target date and volume needs.
- Launch meeting is planned, venue is booked.
- Promotional launch campaign developed (two pieces identified for early PAAB review, and all key promotional tools are in development).
- Pricing submissions are near completion, dialogue with payors is advanced.
- Distribution plan is finalized.

With the above accomplished, the NPP team is at Check-in Point 4 at launch minus three months, at which point senior management will assess launch readiness.

The team will also ensure both external and internal launch milestones have been met.

External Launch Milestones:
- Regulatory timing.
- Payor dialogue: anticipated price and reimbursement versus targets.
- Commercial targets: awareness, anticipated brand usage and forecast update.

Internal Launch Milestones:
- Product supply.
- Tactical execution status versus key issues.

Launch Readiness Review

At this stage, the team performs a Launch Readiness Review (LRR), which identifies launch capability gaps that might slow the product's rapid sales uptake. The review by external consultants will assess a team's preparation of key launch components, including market, product, company, supply, launch timeline and key metrics for success.

Gaps in task execution are identified and addressed in an LRR to establish launch preparedness and clear execution of plans. External consultants facilitate the LRR through one-on-one consultations with launch team members or through the LRR team leader during the bi-weekly/monthly product launch team meetings. The LRR provides the launch team and senior management with confidence regarding preparedness as key issues and assumptions are addressed.

Objectives of Launch Readiness Review

Open Communication
- Provide a clear business review and launch readiness status update to key stakeholder.

- Ensure strategic and tactical alignment between global and company affiliates in other countries.
- Share launch best practices within the organization.

Enhanced Planning
- Improve the launch plan: identify key gaps or risks that the launch team has not addressed in current plan.
- Ensure regular checkpoints to align with launch preparation.
- Check output: identify and track corrective actions.
- Highlight key internal and external launch milestones.
- Ensure pre-and post-launch KPIs are defined and tracked.

Launch Readiness Review Guide

As part of the LRR, actions such as those detailed in the following table must be assessed to verify that key areas are prepared for launch. Take note of each action, then identify any gaps that must be closed.

Table 7 – Launch review guide example

Top Actions	Status	Comments
Brand Team Resourcing and Launch Plan in Place	WIP	Brand Positioning Status Launch Plan Status Budget
Clinical Team Resourcing and Launch Plan in Place	Completed	Staff Position Status Budget Assigned Plan Status
Medical: Confirm Positive Patient Experience	Not started	HQ and Field Medical Obtain Investigator Feedback to Provide a Degree of Confidence
Drug Supply	WIP	Producing at Risk Enables Availability with Short-dated Product

Develop Launch Communication Platform and Leverage Positive Patient Experience	Completed	Status of Project to Develop Complete Platform
Overcome Potential Safety Concerns	Completed	Medical Strategy to Emphasize Safety and Differentiate from Competitor Products
Market Access Plan to Profitably Optimize Patient Access	Completed	Validate Strategy: Market Access Workshop
Multiple Channel Marketing Strategy and Tactics to Optimize Reach and Awareness	WIP	Resources Assigned and Kick-Off Meeting Completed
Legal Team and Strategy in Place to Handle Challenges	WIP	Outline Issues
Promotional Materials Including Vis-Aid, Key Messages etc.	WIP	Kick-off Meeting: Agency
Sales Force: Training, Recruitment and Targeting in Place	WIP	Build on Training and Targeting Work

Suggested Agenda for Review

The LRR should include all aspects of the pre-launch activities and processes. The following table provides a suggested agenda, which will allow time to cover each key area and includes all functional areas, as well as which teams must be involved in the review of each aspect.

Table 8 – Suggested agenda for review

Timing	Functional Area	Lead
8:30–9:00	• Introduction • LRR and Process/Meeting Objectives • Structure, People, Responsibilities, • Roles, Reporting • Executive Summary and Launch • Assumptions, KPI Status	Global and Affiliate LRR Lead LRR Lead Brand Team
9:00–12:15	• LRR Workshop • Launch Team and Organization • Market Overview • Medical Regulatory and Market Access • Brand And Portfolio Strategy • Competitive Overview • KOL and Influencer Development	LRR Lead Brand Med/MA Brand Brand Brand
12:15–12:45	• Lunch	
12:45–16:00	• LRR Workshop • Medical Affairs • Patients and Medical Associations • Communication and PR Programs • Field Force, MSL, KAMs • Partnering/Co-promotion/Co-marketing • Logistics/Operations • Tracking and Performance Management	Medical Brand PR Sales Lead Marketing Supply Brand
16:00–17:00	• LRR Summary • LRR Summary/Debrief Preparation • Debriefing with Affiliate Head and Local Brand Team	Global All

Author's Launch Insights

Hire a consultant to plan and moderate workshop sessions as s/he gathers input for the LRR from all work streams, to allow for a seamless update on launch status. An effective LRR meeting can be accomplished in less than four hours. The final product will provide a thorough review of opportunities and risks, along with strategic recommendations to resolve the identified risks.

SUMMARY OF STRATEGIC CHECK-IN POINT 4

In the approach to Strategic Check-in Point 4, the teams work diligently to develop the company, the product and the market. To ensure the success of the launch, a comprehensive Launch Readiness Review (LRR) is performed as the fourth stage in the overall process.

All functionalities are fully reviewed by an experienced external consulting firm that oversees the LRR. All aspects of the process are checked for accuracy and readiness. They are reviewed and shared in a meeting to ensure that the team is aware of the status of the launch from all functional perspectives. Any gaps found in the LRR must be eliminated before beginning the next stage of readying for the launch.

Once the LRR has been performed and when all the requirements have been met, the team is ready to proceed to **Strategic Check-in Point 5: Launch.**

STRATEGIC CHECK-IN 5:
LAUNCH

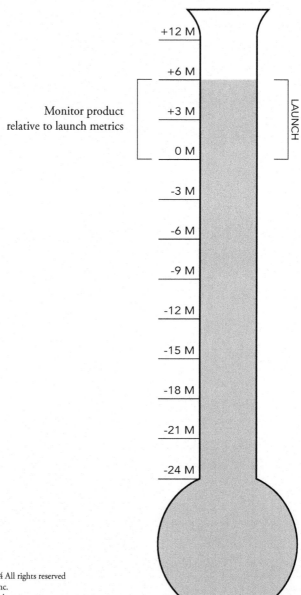

Monitor product
relative to launch metrics

+12 M
+6 M
+3 M
0 M
-3 M
-6 M
-9 M
-12 M
-15 M
-18 M
-21 M
-24 M

LAUNCH

STRATEGIC CHECK-IN POINT 5: LAUNCH

Tasks Initiated in the Three Months Before & After Launch

This check-in point provides the launch team with an early read on how the brand is tracking relative to pre-launch metrics. The team will review a final pre-launch checklist and perform an assessment of internal and external milestones. At the beginning of Check-in Point 5, senior management will assess the status of the launch, including the progress of the brand versus the launch metrics, as well as payor reimbursement versus the targets.

As the launch commences, the team will be tasked with assessing commercial targets, such as sales versus forecast, SOM (share of market), and brand awareness, usage and attitude. During this stage, post-launch message testing will be performed and evaluated.

Key questions to be answered:
1. Are we tracking to excellence?
2. What fine-tuning is needed?
3. How do we accelerate?

The table on the following pages details the tasks to be performed before and during launch.

Table 9 – Tasks to be initiated before and during launch

Item	Tasks	Lead	Timeline
1	Pre-Launch Checklist Review	Marketing/ NPL team	L–3 months

2	NOC Status	Regulatory	L–3 months
3	Establish Launch Meeting Plan	Sales Operations	L–3 months
4	Formulary Submissions (CDR, Quebec and Private Submissions Ready, Pending NOC)	Market Access	L–2 months
5	Determine Final Selling Price	Market Access	L–2 months
6	Pharmacy Distribution Plan	Key Accounts	L–2 months
7	Customer Target Lists by Territory	Sales Effectiveness	L–2 months
8	Update P&L for New Product	Finance	L–2 months
9	Supply Timing Confirmation	Supply	L–2 months
10	Pharmaceutical Advertising Advisory Board Submission	Marketing/ Regulatory	L–2 months
11	Package Label Approvals	QA/Supply/ Regulatory	L–1 months (revise at NOC if needed)
12	Drug Identification Numbers (DINs) Granted	Regulatory	L–5 days
13	Electronic Medical Record Planning Strategy Initiated	Marketing/ Market Access	L–1 month
14	Notice of Compliance (NOC) Received	Regulatory	NOC + 5 days–stage 1 NOC + 6 weeks–stage 2
15	Product Manufactured/ Imported and QC Released	Supply/QA	NOC + 5 days
16	Announce Product Availability	Key Accounts/ Marketing	NOC + 5 days
17	Final Printing of Launch Materials	Marketing	NOC + 5 days
18	Loading Product at Wholesalers	Supply/QA	NOC + 5 days
19	Distribution of Sales Selling Tools	Marketing	NOC + 5 days

20	Date of First Sale	Regulatory/ Market Access/ Sales	NOC + 5 days
21	Sales Force Launch Event	Sales/Marketing/ Management	NOC + 5 days
22	Sales Force Incentive Plan	Sales Effectiveness	NOC + 5 days
23	KOL Launch Symposium	Marketing/CHE	NOC + 5 days
24	Phase IV Trials	Medical/ Marketing Regulatory	Launch
25	Initiate Launch Measurement	Marketing	Ongoing
26	Report Pricing to PMPRB	Market Access	NOC + 1 week for Form 1; Launch + 30 days for Form 2
27	Dating for New Product SKUs	QA	NOC + 5 days

Task 1: Pre-Launch Checklist Review

Responsibility for Decision: NPL Team
Output: Updated launch plan.

Planning Recommendations:

Review final checklist no later than three months prior to launch.

The list on the following pages is reviewed by the launch team work stream lead.

Department Lead: Continuous Health Education
1. Review advocate and speaker development/training programs.
2. Verify that national speaker tours are confirmed.

3. Ensure that Expert Workshops are planned.
4. Check that KOL conferences, symposia and major meetings are booked.
5. Review formal Regional CHE programs, such as interactive problem-or case-based learning workshops, cyber sessions and KOL teleconferences or video conferences.
6. Schedule local hospital and clinic educational events.
7. Representative managed CHE sessions: Are the programs ready and dates booked for CHE?

Department Lead: Finance
1. Develop a budget summary to highlight all costs related to the commercialization activities.
2. Update the P&L statement to reflect any changes in costs or sales projections.

Department Lead: Key Accounts
1. Load orders into distribution channel/warehouses.
2. Ensure that retail stocking and distribution plans are in place.
3. Ensure that hospital and retail pharmacy promotional elements are in place.
4. Review participation and sponsorship of local pharmacy events.

Department Lead: Legal
1. Ensure legal issues, licensing issues and parameters within agreement are addressed.

Department Lead: Market Access
1. Review the pricing strategy. Will PMPRB, CDR, provinces and private payors support the price, and is this in accordance with the forecasted assumptions? Are alternative arguments needed to support the final price?
2. Check PMPRB category as requested.
3. Check product price confirmation from PMPRB.

4. Check reports on status of provincial, third-party and hospital formulary packages.
5. File CDR pre-NOC.
6. File private payor pre-NOC.
7. Prioritize the list of provincial formularies.
8. Check status of third-party administrators.
9. Prioritize list of hospital formularies.
10. Initiate Electronic Medical Record (EMR) product listings.
11. Finalize list price.
12. File post-NOC PMPRB report.
13. Finalize hospital formulary kits.
14. File Institut national d'excellence en santé et en services sociaux (INESSS).

Department Lead: Market Research
1. Assess any significant competitor changes.
2. Probe the experts for their perceptions and expectations of the new product.
3. Determine prescribing intentions: where will this product be placed in their practice, and what products will be displaced?

Department Lead: Marketing
1. Revisit key market issues.
2. Revise the market review and forecast projections to reflect the most recent IMS data.
3. Update the competitor analysis to address any changes in the competitive environment.
4. Ensure the SWOT and critical success factors are still on target.
5. Are the customer's needs and market gaps still valid?
6. Assess strategies and key issues.
7. Make sure that the key market issues are highlighted – they will drive the strategic objectives, strategies and tactics in the commercialization plan.
8. Is the product sales forecast realistic?

9. Elicit expert support as potential advocates for the new product when it is launched.
10. Review regionally-developed KOL activities.
11. Confirm launch supply quantities for trade and sample stock.
12. Regional train-the-trainer programs begin.
13. Post NOC PAAB submission of promotional materials.
14. Ensure PR/media and direct marketing campaigns are in place.
15. Ensure physician promotional elements, such as visual aids, reprints, leave-behind items, audio-visual components and web-based communications, are in place.
16. Ensure product sampling programs are in place.
17. Ensure all sample and promotional material quantities provided.
18. Brainstorm to identify gaps in tactical launch plans to ensure critical success factors are addressed and that brand positioning will be established as planned.

Department Lead: Medical
1. Prepare to initiate studies for Phase IV clinical programs.
2. Check that Physician letters are completed and available.
3. Final hand over of medical KOL clients to sales team.
4. Assess KOL Development with assistance from Marketing.

Department Lead: Regulatory
1. Check timing of submission.
2. Report on first sale.

Department Lead: Sales
1. Launch patient compassionate care program.
2. Recruit additional sales representatives.
3. Assess sales force, ensuring it is identified, on board and trained.
4. Ensure that sales targets and lists are in place.
5. Ensure that bonus plan for sales force is in place.
6. Home training modules completed.
7. Sales team prepared to launch with product monograph and reprints.

Department Lead: Sales Effectiveness
1. Check to determine if more data is needed from the target audience.
2. Assess sales representative capacity requirements.
3. Confirm optimal sales force size and territory configuration.
4. Update customer relationship management software.
5. Purchase sales data form IMS/Brogan.
6. Update expense report modules.
7. Finalize territory business plan template.
8. Launch meeting ready for execution.
9. Sales tools and programs released.
10. Ensure new product is entered into CRM program used by sales team.

Department Lead: Supply
1. Confirm Canadian forecasts with global supply.
2. First Canadian production run after marketing approval granted/NOC.
3. Is the production and packaging schedule on target for the expected launch date?
4. Confirm product sample quantities and timing.
5. Print cartons and labels: DIN received.

Department Lead: Team
1. Get feedback from early communications with review boards and committees.
2. Define challenges and identify with contingency plans.

Task 2: NOC Status

Responsibility for Decision: Regulatory
Output: Check status of the timing of DINs, NOC, monograph and launch date.

Planning Recommendations:

Report on the final steps at TPD and the expected date of NOC and launch. See TPD milestones in the following table for guidance.

Table 10 – Milestone guidance

Task	Item	Timeline	Milestones
1	Log In	Monitor 10 Days Post Submission	*"Acknowledgement of Receipt"* letter issued by TPD should indicate that all appears to be in order.
2	Screening	Monitor 55 Days Post Submission	If NDS is well prepared, *"Acceptance"* letter confirms that it will be accepted for review.
3	Review	Monitor on an ongoing basis	CMC and clinical reviews should be monitored monthly.
4	Clarifaxes	Respond within 10–15 days	RA coordinates the process through the different departments involved in responses.
5	Product Monograph	Negotiate 1 Month Pre-NOC	Negotiation involves several departments, and the process is managed by RA.
6	Labelling	Finalize 2 Weeks Pre-NOC	Finalize through appropriate review process.
7	DIN	Monitor 5 Days Pre-NOC	DINs are usually issued five days pre-NOC.
8	NOC	Day of NOC	Request that NOC be faxed to company immediately.
9	Drug Notification Form	Day of Launch	On the actual day of launch, file Drug Notification Form indicating first sale of the product has taken place.

Task 3: Establish Launch Meeting Plan

Responsibility for Decision: Sales Operations and In-line Marketing
Output: Status report on meeting theme, agenda and venue.

Planning Recommendations:

Planning for the launch meeting should include:
- Meeting theme and special activities.
- Training and scientific elements.
- Launch activities.
- Motivational components.
- Venue and travel specifics.
- Rationale for launch timing – is seasonality an issue with the new product?
- National product launch sales meeting dates and venue.
- National opinion leader launch meeting dates and venue.
- Keynote speakers and chairpersons.

Task 4: Formulary Submission Packages

Responsibility for Decision: Market Access
Output: CDR, submissions ready and pending; report on status of provincial, third-party and hospital formulary packages.

Planning Recommendations:

- Ensure that all is completed and ready for final additions.
- Utilize feedback from the early communications with the drug program staff, review boards and committees.
- Anticipate reactions to the new product.
- Revisit key market issues.

- Upon receipt of NOC and immediately after first sale of product, submit formulary application packages to CDR and private payors. Provincial submissions are to follow CDR's ruling.

Author's Launch Insights

Today, public payors are even more budget conscious and are negotiating confidential listing agreements with brand manufacturers while imposing price cuts on generic drugs too. Reviews of clinical and pharmacoeconomic evidence undertaken by the Common Drug Review, Quebec's Conseil du Medicament, and the Joint Oncology Drug Review are important components of the market access process for new, brand name drugs. The pharmaceutical industry will need to demonstrate cost-effectiveness and respond to payors' expectations for cost sharing when it launches new drugs.

Task 5: Determine Final Selling Price

Responsibility for Decision: Market Access
Output: Price determination as a result of PMPRB, CDR and payor consultations/planning.

Planning Recommendations:

Establish desired pricing based on informed modelling of payor environment.

Pharmaceutical pricing strategies are gaining more public exposure and greater push back as the ceiling for prices gets higher. The Patented Medicine Prices Review Board's (PMPRB) role is primarily price fixing, yet it is not involved in the actual reimbursement decisions. The challenge is that price setting by PMPRB is a central decision, whereas reimbursement is decided at the provincial level.

Task 6: Pharmacy Distribution Plan

Responsibility for Decision: In-line Marketing and Key Accounts
Output: New product information and load forecasts.

Planning Recommendations:

The plan for new product pharmacy distribution should be developed two to four months before launch. The pharmacy plan should include information on chemical name, class and competition. This market research provides the key accounts team with information on potential opportunities and challenges that it may encounter with pharmacies. The distribution plan should also include information on special stocking requirements, such as for auto-shipping, pharmacy programs, advertising, CE sponsorship and budgeting for pharmacy investment.

Perform a forecast of product sales two months before launch. The product sales forecast should be by dosage, province and month from the time of launch up to a period of one year.

Prepare the fact sheet and the fax sheet six to eight weeks before launch. The fax sheet is a notification to wholesalers of the proposed launch. This sheet should contain information on chemical name, class, packing size, storage and shipping requirements, and the expected time of launch. A fact sheet with all available information should then be sent two weeks before the expected launch. Finally, two days before launch, send all of the current information.

Base the retail distribution plan on the product type as you consider the product's market competition. For example, for auto-distribution parts of the plan, limit them to pharmacies in which products have the potential to be switched to a competitor's product.

As for auto-ship plans, any intention to auto-ship the product to key pharmacies should be discussed two to four months before launch. Auto-shipping to stores needs to include extended term payment and a return agreement if the product is not sold after 120 days. Key chains to consider for auto-ship are Shoppers Drug Mart, Katz Group, London Drugs and Sobeys. Pharmacy legislation in some provinces may give pharmacists the power to dispense an alternative generic over a line extension. Be aware that auto-ship is not a preferred model in the industry and should be considered in special cases on a limited basis to avoid significant returns.

Author's Launch Insights

More product loading is not always a good choice for the pharmacy channel. This may lead to significant product write-offs if the product is returned after 60-90 days from hundreds of pharmacies across the country. I recommend loading starting doses only.

Task 7: Customer Target Lists by Territory

Responsibility for Decision: Sales Effectiveness
Output: Territory level target lists for launch

Planning Recommendations:

Develop specialist and primary care target lists for launch. Develop pre-NOC target lists to implement key messaging prior to launch and to facilitate booking appointments with customers prior to the launch.

Author's Launch Insights

Consider pre-booking sales representative appointments to make the first 90 days on territory highly productive. Using sales management input on target list development will allow minor deviation from a head office target list, as sales managers will have insight into prescriber opportunities.

Task 8:
Update Profit & Loss Statement (P&L) for New Product

Responsibility for Decision: Finance
Output: Updated financial forecast.

Planning Recommendations:

Develop a forecast of the expected financial position based on expected conditions and the anticipated operations results and cash flows.

Task 9: Supply Timing Confirmation

Responsibility for Decision: Supply
Output: Confirmation of order with manufacturing; purchase order verification.

Planning Recommendations:

Ensure delivery lead-time is in line with the forecasted NOC date.

Task 10: Pharmaceutical Advertising Advisory Board Submission

Responsibility for Decision: In-line Marketing and Regulatory
Output: Arrange pre-NOC review with PAAB.

Planning Recommendations:

Prior to NOC, when the product monograph negotiations with the Therapeutic Products Directorate (TPD) have reached the final-draft stage, the advertiser or its agency may contact the PAAB to arrange a pre-NOC review. PAAB will accept two advertising promotional systems (APS), and they must be submitted at the same time as sales aids and include one leave-behind, such as a dosage card. More information on PAAB is available in the Appendix.

Task 11: Package Label Approvals

Responsibility for Decision: Quality Assurance, Supply, Regulatory and Marketing

Output:
- Status report on packaging production and on the availability and timing of forecasted launch quantities.
- Packaging artwork drafted and ready with lot number and expiry date.
- All packaging components on hand.
- QA issues resolved.
- Packaging completed and waiting for label to be completed post-DIN approval.

Planning Recommendations:

To minimize the delay between receipt of NOC and stock shipments, labels should ideally be printed in advance and then later overprinted with the DINs.

Author's Launch Insights

When preparing the timeline required to fill the retail and hospital pipeline, consider the additional labour costs of printing DIN over labelling and whether the urgency is necessary. Sometimes supplying product one week post-NOC is acceptable and a rush is not worth the additional costs. A quick cost-benefit analysis will help guide this decision.

Task 12:
Drug Identification Numbers (DINs) Granted

Responsibility for Decision: Regulatory
Output: Provide DINs to QA; supply for package label.

Planning Recommendations:

A different DIN is granted for each separate SKU or variance in the drug strength. Forward DINs to the labelling department as soon as available (approximately two weeks prior to NOC). The launch milestone is to have container labels printed one day after DIN release for immediate launch product labelling and a "date of first sale" for timely formulary submissions.

Task 13:
Electronic Medical Record Planning

Responsibility for Decision: Marketing and Market Access
Output: Establish a system to rapidly gain access to all EMR system drug databases listings.

Planning Recommendations:

Achieving EMR drug listings eliminates a significant barrier to prescribing and lessens a threat to new product sales uptake. Physicians are reluctant to prescribe new products until they are listed on an EMR system where the drug-to-drug, drug-disease and drug-allergy information is identified prior to prescribing a patient's treatment.

Task 14:
Notice of Compliance (NOC) Received

Responsibility for Decision: Regulatory
Output: Provide NOC to all work streams for launch.

Planning Recommendations:

Once NOC is received, marketing may proceed with submitting promotional programs and tools for approval from PAAB.

Task 15:
Product Manufactured/Imported & QC Released

Responsibility for Decision: Supply and Quality Assurance
Output: Product available on time for distribution.

Planning Recommendations:

Monitor supply and QA issues closely to ensure launch plans remain on schedule.

Task 16: Announce Product Availability

Responsibility for Decision: Key Accounts and In-line Marketing
Output: Announce product availability.

Planning Recommendations:

The fact sheet, NOC details, product availability and ordering information should be sent to all wholesalers and pharmacies, Poison Control Centres, drug information centres and CPS. Call all wholesalers to ensure orders are in and that product is shipped once it is available.

Task 17:
Finalize Launch Materials & Programs

Responsibility for Decision: In-line Marketing
Output: Final production of all tactical programs at launch.

Planning Recommendations:

Develop programs but delay printing of them until the product monograph/labelling is approved by TPD. Once completed, conduct a final review of all materials once the final PM is available.

Suggested initial launch toolkit for sales team:
- Detail aid/Sales aid.
- HCP announcement letter.
- Dosage Card.
- MOA video.
- Exhibit panels/booth.
- Patient material.
- Objection handlers.
- Update website.
- Distribute conference calendar and strategies.
- e-CPS update.
- Full Product Monograph (PM.)

- Clinical studies.
- e-Samples, traditional samples and recommended sample allocation plan.
- e-CHE program including, slide kit.

Task 18: Loading Product at Wholesalers

Responsibility for Decision: Supply and Quality Assurance
Output: Stocked wholesalers.

Planning Recommendations:

Ship the product to wholesalers within a week of receipt of the NOC.

Author's Launch Insights

Consider the time required for implementation when developing sales programs for the field. Often, marketing teams develop too many programs, assuming that customers will become fatigued by a given sales tool. However, selling is about frequency, and this likely means using the same tools again and again.

Task 19: Distribution of Sales Selling Tools

Responsibility for Decision: Marketing
Output: Sales materials shipped to sales representatives before launch.

Planning Recommendations:

Prepare a launch kit for each sales rep and provide specific training as to how to implement each program.

Task 20: Date of First Sale

Responsibility for Decision: Regulatory, Market Access and Sales
Output: Required record of first sale.

Planning Recommendations:

Indicate the year, month and day when the drug product is first sold in Canada, whether it is following issuance of NOC, a special access program, a clinical trial application or as an investigational new drug.

The record of the first sale of the product is required for formulary submissions. Provide copies of NOC, Drug Identification Numbers (DINs) and the "date of first sale" document to market access for inclusion in PMPRB, CDR, Quebec, and private payor formulary submissions.

Task 21: Sales Force Launch Event

Responsibility for Decision: Marketing, Sales Management
Output: Motivated and well-trained sales team.

Planning Recommendations:

The launch meeting should be the culmination of an extended, distance-learning training program. This is where representatives will receive final directions on the promotional strategy. Also, any final training can be completed, and the necessary motivational message can be sent from the session leaders and the brand team.

Author's Launch Insights

Launch meetings need to build confidence in sales representatives. Some of the best training at a launch comes from physician discussions regarding diagnosis and treatment of the condition in question, along with information about where your new product could fit in a physician's choice of treatments.

Task 22: Sales force Incentive Plan

Responsibility for Decision: Sales Effectiveness
Output: Sales incentive program.

Planning Recommendations:

The incentive program should include elements that reward both results and the activities required to achieve the results (i.e.. key message delivery, hospital formulary status achieved).

Product launch incentives are a wonderful idea, yet if formulary and EMR systems are not aligned with the incentive opportunity, the sales incentive can become a disincentive too. Align the incentive with the opportunity in the sales environment in an effort to drive behavioural change for the right type of patients, and initially the right type of physician targets: innovators and early adopters.

Task 23: KOL Launch Symposium

Responsibility for Decision: In-line Marketing, Medical, Regulatory and CHE planning
Output: Final details for launch symposium with KOLs from advisory board as keynote speakers.

Planning Recommendations:

Use KOL input to finalize the details for the symposium because, as part of a phase IV program, it will have a significant impact on recruiting physicians to participate in the phase IV trials.

Task 24: Phase IV Trials

Responsibility for Decision: Medical, Regulatory, Market Access and Marketing
Output: Phase IV trials with appropriate pharmacoeconomics endpoints.

Planning Recommendations:

Utilize Phase IV trials for pharmacoeconomic benefit in order to facilitate listings on key formularies.

Task 25: Initiate Launch Measurement

Responsibility for Decision: In-line Marketing and Market Research
Output: Track launch performance and complete any research necessary for positioning or messaging adjustments.

Planning Recommendations:

Support the continued success of the brand via regular performance tracking metrics and current and future opportunity analysis.

Perform secondary data-source monitoring of the product's performance tracking using key indicators, including:
- Market growth, market penetration and share (total dollars and number of prescriptions).
- Competitor activity and response to new product launch.
- Regulatory, pricing and reimbursement issues.
- Variances to forecast and budget on key indicators.
- Quantitative post-detailing research with customers to assess detailing and message effectiveness.
- Quantitative post-launch monitoring research with customers (prescribers and patients), **Components to include measurement of:**
  a. Product awareness, trial and usage.
  b. Product satisfaction and performance against expectations.
  c. The competitive set of key attributes/behavioural drivers.

d. Identification of perceived product strengths, weaknesses and competitive differences.

- Qualitative research amongst prescribers and non-prescribers (patients and physicians, respectively) to identify key barriers to trial and usage among non-prescribers.
- Exploration of opportunities to leverage perceived strengths among prescribers with non-prescribers.
- Qualitative promotional material development and testing (if required).

Task 26: Report Pricing to PMPRB

Responsibility for Decision: Market Access and Regulatory
Output: Submission of forms 1 and 2 to PMPRB.

Planning Recommendations:

It is essential to ensure that submissions are on schedule and that they include the product monograph and selling price.

Form 1: Submit within seven days after issuance of an NOC or first sale in Canada, whichever comes first.

Form 2: Submit when drug is first offered for sale in Canada. The data for the first day of sale must be provided no later than thirty days after the date of first sale.

(source: **www.pmprb-cepmb.gc.ca/english/home.asp?x=1**)

Task 27: Dating for New Product SKUs

Responsibility for Decision: Quality Assurance
Output: Extended dating for new product SKUs.

Planning Recommendations:

To minimize product expiry risk, the marketer needs to push for extended dating post-launch to avoid issues with sales forces managing the dating of expired product. Stability data becomes available once the product has spent time on the market. The costs to the QA department to continue testing in order to extend stability data are significantly less than the costs to have representatives in the field removing expired product from customer offices and pharmacies, which should be minimized to avoid creating a negative perception of the brand.

SUMMARY OF STRATEGIC CHECK-IN POINT 5

During Strategic Check-in Point 5, the teams make all the final preparations for the launch, beginning no later than three months prior to launch and running up to the days before and after receipt of the NOC. After two years of working toward launch success, the launch is initiated during this stage after ensuring that submissions, packaging, distribution, pricing, timeline and sales teams are prepared. Announcements and reports are made during the launch period, and then work begins to assess the launch's metrics, to initiate phase IV trials and to collect data to extend dating on the product.

By three months post-launch, the following must be in place:
- Promotion is underway per tactical plan.
- External launch metrics are available for review, including:
    a. Ex-factory sales have been registered.
    b. One month of TSA sales and TRx data is available.
    c. Initial wave of message testing has been conducted and data is available.
    d. Brand awareness, usage and attitude have been measured in key targets.
    e. Market access plan is underway, and progress is evident.

If all the above initiatives are in place, then the team is ready to proceed to **Strategic Check-in Point 6: Launch Effectiveness.**

STRATEGIC CHECK-IN 6:
LAUNCH EFFECTIVENESS

Assess success of launch versus
metrics established during pre-launch

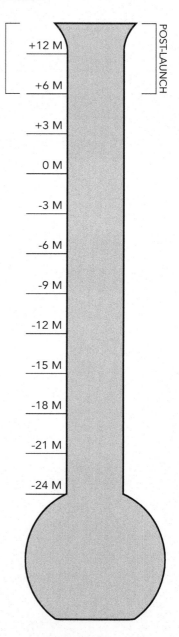

POST-LAUNCH

+12 M

+6 M

+3 M

0 M

-3 M

-6 M

-9 M

-12 M

-15 M

-18 M

-21 M

-24 M

STRATEGIC CHECK-IN POINT 6: LAUNCH EFFECTIVENESS

Tasks Initiated Between Launch & Six Months Post-Launch

Key questions to be addressed at Strategic Check-in Point Six:
1. How do we accelerate the current launch trajectory?
2. Did we achieve launch excellence?
3. What are the key launch learnings?

For the majority of pharmaceutical launches, the product's trajectory is set within the first six months of launch. Brand teams often have limited insight on what is happening on the ground, or their insight may be gained too late to be helpful. For example, the launch uptake can vary by more than 30% from region to region.

The primary focus of this review is to assess the success of the launch against the metrics established pre-launch. This captures the key lessons, successes and gaps to improve organizational performance and launch capabilities. This internal review should capture input from all launch stakeholders, including medical, marketing, market access, regulatory, supply, QA, sales and training.

For optimal launch success, an organization must have the ability to develop broad insights into launch performance and to translate those insights into quick actions to correct deviations from plans and projections.

To enhance launch capabilities, an organization needs:
1. Real-time data monitoring and automated data feeds that synchronize information.
2. Information that is tailored to the brand priorities

(A, B or C) which were established during the initial stages of the commercial assessment.

3. Information that provides visual integration of various data sources and systems.

4. Analysis of prescriptions, perceptions and behaviors at the patient and physician level.

5. Quick decisions that use real time insights based on integrated prescriber, patient and field force data, as well as a quick understanding of the underlying market drivers for the purposes of a shorter response time.

The following section details the tasks to be completed during Check-in Point 6: Launch Effectiveness. The following table lists the tasks, responsible parties and the timeline for the completion of each task.

Table 11: Tasks to be initiated at launch through six months post-launch

Item	Task	Lead	Timeline
1	Establish Performance Measures for Course Correction	Launch Team	L–0 to L+6
2	Promotion is Underway per Tactical Plan	Marketing	L+0
3	Ex-Factory Sales Registered	Sales Analytics	L+1
4	Message Testing	Market Research	L+3 to L+6
5	Formulary Listings Achieved	Market Access	L+6
6	EMR Listings Achieved	Marketing/ Market Access	L+6
7	Medical Support	Medical	L+0 to L+6
8	External Launch Metrics are Available for Review	Launch Analytics	L+0 to L+12
9	Launch Effectiveness Review	Consultant	L+12

Task 1:
Establish Performance Metrics for Course Correction

Responsibility for Decision: Launch team including: Sales Analytics, Marketing, Market Research and outside Consultants.
Output: A system to accurately measure key launch performance dynamics.

Planning Recommendations:

Develop a launch dashboard with customized visuals, including top-down geographic views to monitor and support the launch team's ability to react more quickly. Within these visuals, set up a monitoring system that alerts for potential risks or market opportunities. This will enable dynamic decision-making and the ability to clearly understand customer behaviour. Dashboards allow for rapid understanding of underlying performance drivers by integrating the most relevant data. Rapid adjustment of commercial activities is possible with the constant monitoring of market changes and with a dedicated team for customizing the system to allow for a deeper understanding of launch metrics.

The monitoring system should include the following:
- Competitive performance: sales volume, patient switching, patient or prescriber segmentation.
- Sales key performance indicators: number of visits, number of samples distributed, CHE completed.
- Market feedback: awareness or perception levels regarding safety, usages, adherence, compliance and loading.
- An established warning system: identifying under performance areas and performing analysis of causes.

Task 2:
Promotion is Underway per Tactical Plan

Responsibility for Decision: Marketing and Sales Force
Output: Implementation of tactical plan.

Planning Recommendations:

Sales team buy-in is essential for effective implementation of tactical programs. Obtain input from key individuals involved in program implementation to ensure understanding of each program's objectives and their relationships to strategies. This additional involvement increases participation and improves implementation success rates. It is also helpful to measure the implementation of a program and to hold the team members accountable for the desired results.

Author's Launch Insights

To ensure sales programs are implemented effectively, invest more time on actual program implementation discussion at sales meetings to ensure that the sales force understands program objectives and desired outcomes. Too many times, marketers gloss over programs and the sales force never really grasps program implementation and expected outcomes. I often asked sales managers and sales representatives to provide the program introductions at sales meetings. They then became the program ambassadors, fielding questions from sales representatives. Buy-in can increase dramatically when a rep introduces the program, with the project owner from marketing ensuring that the program is rolled out appropriately.

Task 3: Ex-Factory Sales Registered

Responsibility for Decision: Sales Analytics
Output: Sales volume is provided to IMS/Brogan for tracking purposes.

Planning Recommendations:

Register ex-factory sales for the purpose of accurately tracking sales across therapeutic levels and to obtain an accurate understanding of market dynamics.

Task 4: Message Testing

Responsibility for Decision: Market Research
Output: Benchmarked measures compared to prior measures in order to monitor market changes to messaging.

Planning Recommendations:

To test the effectiveness of the product's messaging with physicians, the research will include:
- Measurement of product awareness, trial and usage.
- Measurement of product satisfaction and performance against prior expectation and against the competitive set of key attributes/behavioural drivers.
- Identification of perceived product strengths, weaknesses and competitive differentiation.
- Qualitative research among prescribers and non-prescribers to:
  a. Identify key barriers to trial and usage among non-prescribers.
  b. Explore opportunities to leverage perceived strengths among prescribers and non-prescribers.

- Qualitative promotional material development and testing (if required).

Track launch performance and complete any research necessary for positioning and messaging adjustments.

Task 5: Formulary Listings Achieved

Responsibility for Decision: Market Access
Output: Formulary listing status and expected listing updates with targeted payors.

Planning Recommendations:

When government or third-party payors refuse to reimburse a drug, then the lack of private and public formulary reimbursements may, depending on the target market, result in little customer interest to prescribe. For most new products to succeed, it is imperative to gain formulary listing support from key stakeholders.

Task 6: EMR Listings Achieved

Responsibility for Decision: Market Access and Marketing
Output: Clearly understand the impact of delayed listings to launch uptake using EMR listing services.

Planning Recommendations:

The commercial team needs to focus on gaining early listings on EMR systems to remove a potential roadblock to prescribing.

Task 7: Medical Support

Responsibility for Decision: Medical
Output: Establishing on-going medical role by continuing relationship development and support of KOLs.

Planning Recommendations:

The medical team's focus on relationship development and support of KOLs by MSLs is most valuable to clinical development, yet medical offers a significant role in the development of a product's success focusing on the following: identification of new KOLs, responding to requests for product information, relationship development/support of investigators, delivering presentations and speeches, supporting investigator initiated trials, gathering and reporting competitive intelligence and supporting KOL research interests, KOL speaker training, presenting pharmacoeconomic data for market access and moderating advisory boards are a few considerations for continued medical support via MSLs. .

Task 8:
External Launch Metrics are Available for Review

Responsibility for Decision: Launch Team
Output:
- Report on external launch metrics, including commercial targets and payor reimbursement versus targets.
- Report on internal launch milestones, including KOL, MD participation in CHE, sales call metrics and the status of hospital formulary listings.

- Identification of key learnings from the measurement of milestones.

Planning Recommendations:

The following are the suggested key metrics for review:
- External metrics.
- Commercial targets.
- KOL and physician awareness metrics.
- Payor access metrics Patient acceptance metrics.
- Adverse events and regulatory metrics.
- Internal metrics.
- Sales force performance metrics.
- Corrective action determination metrics.
- Critical launch success factors metrics.
- Post-launch target recalibration metrics.

Task 9: Launch Effectiveness Review

Responsibility for Decision: Consultant and Launch Team
Output: Gain feedback from key internal stakeholders to identify future launch performance improvements.

Planning Recommendations:

The launch effectiveness review is not a review of launch team members; individual performance measures need to be embedded in the company's employee review system. The intent of this review is to measure the processes and the performance of the launch product. This review is key to ensuring that launch success is maintained by finding possible improvements in the process and organizational successes.

As part of the review to measure launch effectiveness and to improve the organization's future performance, address these key process questions at twelve months post-launch:

a. Is there an established launch process that identifies the key tasks for a successful launch within the organization to guide cross-functional launch teams?

b. To support the need for clear senior management support and direction, does senior management engage in developing launch strategy during the commercial assessment stage?

c. As key learnings develop out of various markets, does the organization share launch insights from first-wave to second-wave countries?

d. What bottlenecks within the organization negatively affected the launch teams?

e. Are there clear measures in regards to launch readiness for future launches in key markets?

f. How is innovation fostered in the organization to maximize profitability?

g. Based on the launch results, does the organization clearly have expertise in launching new products?

h. Does the organization document launch tasks and key activities?

Next, review the product's launch performance, addressing these key questions:

a. How did this launch perform in regards to industry benchmarks, sales volumes (dollar sales and total prescription sales) market share and profitability, on the sixth month uptake?

b. Were course correction activities and measures effective?

c. How did the product's launch perform in comparison to the original expectations?

d. How effective was the implementation of the launch positioning and strategy?

e. How will the next product launch impact the organization's growth and profitability?

SUMMARY OF STRATEGIC CHECK-IN POINT 6

Post-launch, the following must be in place:
- All promotion is underway per tactical plan.
- External launch metrics are available for review.
- Ex-factory sales have been registered.
- Ten months of TSA sales and TRx data are available.
- Second wave of message testing has been conducted and data is available.
- Brand awareness, usage and attitude have been measured in key targets.
- Formulary listings have been achieved as per plans.
- EMR listings have been achieved as per plan.

With the above as inputs, the NPP team is at Strategic Check-in Point 6 at L+12 months, where senior management will assess:
- Launch status, specifically the progress of brand versus launch metrics.
- **External launch milestones:**
  a. **Commercial targets** – sales vs. forecast, share of market, brand awareness, brand usage and attitude, post-launch message testing (wave two).
  b. **Payors** – reimbursement vs. targets.

- **Internal launch milestones:**
  a. Number of KOLs and MDs participating in CHE, sales call metrics, status of hospital formulary listings.
  b. Key launch learning: applicable to other launches.

At the end of **Strategic Check-in Point 6: Launch Effectiveness**, the team has implemented a detailed launch process that resulted in proper preparation and planning, a successful and timely launch of the new product, continual product success and integrated process knowledge for future product launches.

APPENDIX

Support Information

This section was created to offer more detail based on functional work stream responsibilities and additional launch references. Each organization will have different processes, yet this section offers a high-level overview for the reader.

APPENDIX CONTENTS

Advertising & Public Relations Agency Briefs

Agency Brief

Advertising and/or public relations agencies are valued partners for a launch. An agency brief is a document issued to an advertising agency, graphic designer or other similar communications company. This document conveys the objectives, timescales and responsibilities for producing a communication program, and assists in the selection of an agency of record (AOR).

- Confidentiality – no brief must ever be submitted to any outside service provider without a legally endorsed NDA (non-disclosure agreement).
- Integrity – where possible, exclude material of a financially sensitive nature and submit the brief to the corporate communications team for pre-approval. Avoid "spinning" content. The brief is not a PR document, but a clear and accurate overview of the product's opportunities and issues to build a positive PR response.
- Relevance – The brief should be geared towards framing the issues and opportunities that the agency will realistically support. Where an agency's past performance is unknown, request references or establish a "pay-for-performance" approach. Results are the key here.

A comprehensive PR brief should include as many of the following points as possible:
- Background – what has led you to this campaign or project?
- Communications objectives – what are the specific goals you want to achieve through communications activity?

- Target audiences – who are you aiming to influence or engage? Define! Do you know how you want to reach your audiences?
- Messages – what do you want them to understand or believe as a result of your communications work?
- Potential challenges – are you aware of any difficulties that will need to be addressed?
- Timelines – when do you want activities to occur? How long is the timeline to prepare?
- Budget – how much does your company need to spend? This may affect the choice of activities.
- Evaluate – as you develop the program or tactic, consider how activity will be measured for success?
- Identify the best communication channels: radio, television, newspaper etc.
- Have you trained and coached KOL/GP speakers for media interviews, in French and English, and regionally, in order to leverage the brand's positioning?

Creative Brief

The creative brief is a written document that concisely summarizes the business and creative requirements for a specific project or relationship. It is not a proposal, request for proposal (RFP) or initiation form. It details the overriding business objectives and digs deep into a project, identifying the main factors that drive the entire creative strategy.

A poorly prepared creative brief can become a hindrance more than a driving force in the design process. If half-heartedly put together without the input of key stakeholders, it can actually muddle a project's overarching goals, sabotaging any real chance for success.

Conversely, a well-written brief will contribute to robust business results and a more cohesive and efficient creative process. This design brief is a written agreement, or contract, between the parties involved with the project.

Creative briefs should be used for any design project, no matter how small. Examples of large-scope projects include advertising campaigns, branding, logo development, naming, packaging, integrated communications programs, website projects and virtually all tactical programs.

Key categories of the brief include:

Background information on company and product: introduce the project and any background information that will drive its progress (e.g. new products, positioning strategies). Ideally, the vendor/partner will already understand the company, product or service before the creative brief process has begun, so this section can be short.

1. Patient and target audience groups – identify the gender, age, geographic location, characteristics, priorities, occupations, and cultural considerations for each group. Find out what motivates and inspires each group, and identify differences and similarities between the sub-groups.

2. Brand attributes, opportunity, proof, promise, and mission – brand equity, assets, and strengths, primary and secondary brand attributes, differentiators, expected brand perceptions and adjectives are included here.

3. Competitive landscape – refer to the corporate website or research you have collected; analyze the competitive landscape, chart strengths and weaknesses, and determine how these are relevant to what you will be developing for the client.

4. Best practices – inspirational (i.e. what does the product team like and why? How is it relevant?).

5. Business objectives (success criteria) – pinpoint the goals in developing a particular piece or service (i.e. is the initiative meant to increase awareness, generate sales leads or educate existing physicians?).

6. Creative strategies – outline existing brand guidelines (i.e. what is relevant and what isn't?), logo, color palette, typography, imagery, content requirements, claims, information hierarchy, visual and editorial themes, tone and image. This is where subjective opinions turn into objective strategies. A relevant question: if your agency can provide out-of-the-box solutions, how would they define this further?

7. Functionality specifications – required for online program components.

8. Comparisons – how the audience should perceive the brand/ product/service?

9. Contribution and approval process – which contributors get involved at what stage of the project and what are they expected to contribute and/or approve?

10. Testing requirements – define how you test during the project and then, after it is completed, measure its success.

11. Training requirements – establish and gain buy-in from sales force for program materials.

12. Timeline – describe shelf life, NOC/launch target dates, how long the program will be used with customers.

13. Budget – the financial commitment to the endeavour and how much effort the agency will invest.

Continuing Medical Education (CME) Overview

The role of continuing medical education, its effectiveness in driving appropriate prescribing, and its impact on the success of a pharmaceutical product is an important and evolving one. As a product passes through the various stages of its life cycle, the educational needs of customers change, and so must the objectives of education within the tactical mix.

Pre-launch

Educational Objective: Provide high-science education to early adopters.

Simultaneously, collaborating with these KOLs to understand the educational needs of the market in preparation for launch is critical. Using pre-launch educational initiatives to prepare advocates and speakers for launch will create a seamless approach to education.

It is important to note that educational initiatives prior to receiving a NOC may not be promotional in nature. These educational initiatives should never be seen as sales-related efforts in support of your product prior to receiving NOC.

Introduction (Launch)

Educational Objective: Provide practical education to high-prescribing physicians.

At launch, large-scale educational efforts are required. Providing various educational formats that satisfy the different learning preferences of individual physicians is important, with a focus on answering key questions. Material presentation and support from well-known and respected KOLs will be critical to the success of these programs.

At this stage, prescribing physicians must learn:

1. WHO – is the ideal patient for this product?
2. WHAT – does the scientific data say to support its use?
3. WHERE – does the product fit in with my current choice of therapies (i.e. what will be displaced)?
4. WHY – would I use this product over what I am currently using?
5. HOW – do I safely and effectively use/prescribe this product?

Data Services Organizations

IMS Brogan Data Services

Application that allows for the following data to be run:

Canadian Compuscript

CompuScript measures the retail outflow of prescriptions, or the rate at which drugs move out of pharmacies into the hands of consumers via formal prescriptions. CompuScript measures what is dispensed by the pharmacist to the consumer.

CompuScript is frequently used for tracking, forecasting, and strategic planning to allow analysts to study the following:

- Prescription volume, market share, and trend.
- Prescription prices paid by the consumer.
- Prescription characteristics.
- Share of prescription activity by province.
- Share of prescription activity generated by different physician specialties.
- Reports can be run by USC, molecule, combined molecule, specialty, province or any combination of the aforementioned items.

- Application has the most current five years of data available; historical data for selected markets is available through the Strategic Market Research department.
- Monthly updates occur on the 18th of each month (e.g. September updates are available on the 18th of October).

Canadian Drugstore and Hospital Sales (CDH)

Canadian drugstore and hospital sales can be run as a total sales amount or split between drugstore and hospital outlets.

Reports can be run by USC, molecule, combined molecule or province.

Unlike TSA data, CDH data offers a comparative look at multiple competitors and markets. TSA Competitive data only lists grouped competitor sales (in broad categories, such as 'SSRI Competitors'); CDH data displays sales for each individual competitor.

Application has the most current five years of data available.

Monthly updates occur on the 25th of each month (e.g. September updates are available on the 25th of October). The data can be subscribed to on a quarterly basis.

Canadian Promotional Audit (CPA)

CPA data allows for the running of promotional data for any promoted brand.

Data options include: total cost of promotion, cost of detailing, cost of journal advertisements, number of journal ads, number of details, detail position, details with sample units.

Data can be run by province and by specialty.

Application has the most current five years of data available.

Canadian Disease and Therapeutic Index (CDTI)

CDTI data records the therapeutic use of prescription and non-prescription medications by office-based physicians, as well as from medical visits that do not involve drug therapy, such as routine check-ups and consultations.

CDTI data can be used to:
- Determine market size and characteristics by diagnosis.
- Determine areas for long-term research and short-term development.
- Examine diagnosis profiles for information relevant to clinical testing.
- Target physician specialties to promote.
- Monitor usage and treatment patterns by drug and by physician specialty.
- CDTI data is updated quarterly. A helpful an appealing option may be to subscribe only to the Q1 (March) and Q3 (September) quarters.

Xponent/DLD Data

Prescriber-level prescription information.

TRx and NRx, decile ranking, share and average Rx volume for identified products and markets.

Data is only available for DLD provinces (Alberta, Saskatchewan, Ontario, Quebec, New Brunswick, Nova Scotia).

NBRx (New to Brand) Data

Research has shown the New-to-Brand Rx data is an indicator of brand performance, particularly during product launches.

Key metrics offered by NBRx include: new to brand volume (NBRx) of prescriptions generated by new patients, switches and add-ons, and brand volume continuation of refill and new Rx.

TSA (Territory Sales Analysis) Data

Tracks the sales of selected pharmaceutical manufacturers' products to retail pharmacies, dispensing physicians, nursing homes, hospitals and other purchasers. Sales data for Strategic products are available at the National, Regional, Territory, FSA and Outlet levels.

Data is available monthly (around the 20th of the month)

TSA Competitive Data

Tracks the competitive sales of selected pharmaceutical manufacturers' products to retail pharmacies, dispensing physicians, nursing homes, hospitals and other purchasers.

To meet competitive confidentiality requirements, competitive products must be grouped into product buckets (i.e. Paxil is not listed individually but is included in the SSRI Competitors bucket).

Data is available quarterly.

TPA (Territory Prescription Analysis) Data

Provides TRx and NRx data of various markets at the National, Regional, Territory and FSA levels.

Market Profiler

Web-based application used to provide counts of prescribers by specialty by province.

Includes:
- Market/Brand Analysis (total number of prescribers by market/ brand by decile by province/national); Specialty Analysis (identifying specialist writers in a market); Cross Tab Analysis (count of overlap physicians in two markets by decile).

Data is updated quarterly and is only available for DLD provinces (Alberta, Saskatchewan, Ontario, Quebec, New Brunswick and Nova Scotia).

Physician Contact Lists

Provides the option of a contact list without having to purchase DLD data.

List is generated based on our specific requests (such as D1 and D2 CCB prescribers in Ontario).

Rx Dynamics

Using patient claims data, Rx Dynamics tracks share, patients, first-line patients and tabulates gains and losses due to switching among specific products.

Customizing table options are also available (for example, dosing or concomitant therapies).

Available for both private payor and public payor (ODB) environments.

Monthly data is available.

Pharmastat

Provides drug plan sales intelligence on almost every prescription drug marketed in Canada.

The Pharmastat database includes 100% of public data in most provinces plus NIHB. Private coverage is estimated at 67%.

Pharmastat data can be used to:
- Identify market trends
- Estimate market size
- Analyses for formulary submissions

iMAM

Reports the latest adjustments to all Canadian provincial formularies and NIH, and is updated weekly.

iMAM can be used to:
- Keep current on formulary activities.
- Get accurate and timely competitive intelligence.
- Retrieve formulary and AQPP price information.
- Monitor price changes.
- Rx Ticker Provides the most current drug product sales.

Other Data Services

- FirstWord Email subscription service that documents pharmaceutical industry updates as they happen (e.g. merger news, research developments, pipeline information, product recalls, shareholder updates).
- Executive Plus option allows subscribers to look up historical information.
- Statistics Canada.
- Various free and for-purchase items research available via the Statistics Canada website: www.statca.gc.ca.
- Government and Industry Trade publications.
- Data Monitor Reports.
- Competitor CHE and promotional materials.

- Patient support group publications.
- Competitive intelligence reports.
- Medical publications.
- Company websites.

Pharma Launch Inc. Data Services

EMR drug database listings are a leading performance indicator of new product launch sales uptake for all pharmaceutical products. Achieving EMR drug listings eliminates a significant barrier to prescribing and a threat to new product sales uptake. Physicians are reluctant to prescribe new products until new products are listed on an EMR system where the drug-to-drug, drug-disease and drug-allergy information is identified prior to prescribing a patient's treatment. Pharma Launch Inc. offers an EMR accelerator service to gain listings more quickly and to eliminate a barrier to prescribing. www.PharmaLaunch.ca

Finance Overview

To measure the cost effectiveness of a launch, it is important to set up project, SKU (Stock Keeping Unit), and product cost centres. At the early stages, a project number can be used to track expenses. Once product SKU numbers are available, product codes can be established. The following section outlines key finance tasks for a new product launch. It is also very important to inform your finance partner regarding the timing of the launch to allow sufficient time to set up accounts for the tracking of expenses and sales.

1. Set up Project Number – Project Number will act as a cost collector for any and all expenses incurred related to product launch prior to SKU and department set-up in your enterprise software system.

2. Update the Preliminary P&L Statement for the New Product – the profit and loss statement (P&L) is also referred to as an income statement, earnings statement, operating statement or statement of operations. It is a company's financial statement that indicates how the revenue (money received from the sale of products and services before expenses are taken out – the "top line") is translated into the net income (the result after all revenues and expenses have been accounted for – the "bottom line"). It displays the revenues recognized for a specific period and the cost and expenses charged against these revenues, including write-offs (such as depreciation and amortization of various assets) and taxes. The purpose of the income statement is to demonstrate whether the company/brand has made or lost money for the reported period. The income statement represents a period of time.

3. Develop P&L – the P&L statement relies on the market assessment and forecast, product forecast, term sheet and assumptions related to the manufacturing, distribution, sales and marketing costs for the new product. The currency impact must also be considered in terms of forecasting for a standard foreign exchange adjustment.

4. New SKU in Financial System – set up new product SKUs in the financial reporting system used within organization.

5. New Department – the department refers to the Brand Unique Identifier (Profit Centre / Cost Centre), similar to the Project Number, when it captures all the expenses related to the brand. In addition, the department number captures all revenue associated with the brand. Each brand will have a department code that provides transparency on the profitability of the brand by itemizing revenues, costs and expenses related to the brand.

6.   Supply Contract – supply Contract in terms of dating.

7.   Standard Costing (Internal and External Costs) – cost of product including mark up costs.

8.   Currency Requirements – Will there be need for a standard adjustment?

9.   Vendor Set Up – Lead Times: for demand planning.

10.   Lot Sizes – Establish lot sizes required for demand planning.

11.   Inventory Management – is there inventory to be transferred? What is the value of the inventory? Are there additional packaging requirements?

12.   Accounting Updates in Terms of Reporting – ensuring all monthly and quarterly processes and documents related to product are captured in the accounting department. All journal entries and account reconciliations and schedules (such as returns, gross margin and obsolescence) should capture and include the new brand.

13.   Sales force Allocation – determine position of product (1st, 2nd or 3rd) and financial impact on new brand and other brands in strategic portfolio. Consider the impact of any additional head count.

Key Account Overview

Key accounts, including wholesalers and pharmacy chains, need to be managed effectively for timely distribution of information upon first sale and product availability. A successful new product launch will require:

- A timeline with critical elements four months before projected launch. It should contain details of expected date of NOC, launch, fact sheet, and fax sheet for pharmacy customers.
- Distribution plan developed over 4–6 months.
- Details on the product type (solid, liquid), special transportation, storage requirements, general pharmacy or specialty market should be provided. This will help plan and coordinate with wholesalers.
- New product information developed approximately 3–4 months before launch.
- A fact sheet is a notification of the proposed launch to wholesalers and contains the product's chemical name, class, packing size, storage and shipping requirements and expected time of launch. A fact sheet with all available information will be provided upon approval.
- This information will help key account teams understand and identify market opportunities and challenges with the distribution channels. In addition, strategies are required for distribution, along with decisions for special stocking requirements such as auto shipments to pharmacies, developing pharmacy tactics (advertising, CHE sponsorship where allowed), and establishing budgets for pharmacy investments.
- Product sales forecast 3–6 months before launch by dosage, province, and month from the time of launch for a period of one year.

Market Access Overview

Market access is likely the most important variable in a product lifecycle; from a new product launch to negotiating an exclusive tendered contract post-genericization. Historically, reimbursement has been achieved close to the launch of a product and then set aside to focus on marketing and sales.

Beginning with the development of a strong value proposition, communicating that proposition effectively and building stakeholder support throughout the product lifecycle for payors are key components in any market access strategy. Depending on the target market, without private and public formulary reimbursement, sales efforts and customer interest in the new drug are of little value when government or third-party payors refuse to reimburse a drug. This section will provide the reader an understanding of the market access process in a product's lifecycle.

Key components of market access components in a lifecycle strategy will be:
- Maximizing the success of early stage development and regulatory activities for future reimbursement support.
- Building a strong value proposition for payors throughout the product life cycle.
- Communicating effectively to win support from key stakeholders.
- Maintaining reimbursement success through ongoing marketing activities.

Patented Medicine Pricing Review Board (PMPRB)

Early informal discussions and consultation with PMPRB are critical elements to develop an appropriate pricing strategy. The Board staff will help manufacturers determine appropriate comparator drugs to build models for different price tests, depending on the level of therapeutic improvement that the Board will later determine.

Development of the New Medicine Submission to the PMPRB comes much later in the process; an appropriate pricing objective must be formulated, however, at the beginning of the process.

PMPRB classifies new products into four levels of therapeutic improvement.
1. Breakthrough – International Median Test.

2. Substantial improvement – Higher of Therapeutic Class Comparison Test or International Median Test.

3. Moderate improvement – Midway between Therapeutic Class Comparison Test and International Median Test.

4. Slight or no improvement – Therapeutic Class Comparison Test or Reasonable Relationship Test (for line extensions).

The classification is done based on head-to-head Phase III trials that should compare the new product with the most used/highest priced available comparator.

The slight or no improvement level allows for little or no price flexibility. If a product can be developed as a unique entity or significant advance in therapy, it will produce a moderate or substantial improvement submission, which must be considered an objective during the protocol design for Phase III trials.

If a breakthrough, substantial or moderate designation appears unlikely, Phase III trials should be designed to maximize the primary indication and dosage wording in the labelling.

In preparation for the New Medicine Submission to the PMPRB, begin to collect the following information:

Assessment of relevant published and unpublished scientific information and clinical practice guidelines related to the new product, and the disease or condition for which it will be prescribed.

Identify all other drugs that are used for the new product's indication.

Make note of all properties that differentiate the new product from competitors, taking into account primary and secondary factors, as defined by PMPRB guidelines.

Collect the comparator's prices in the six sources of prices indicated by PMPRB: OPDP, RAMQ, AQPP, McKesson, IMS and PPS.

Collect the international prices of the new product in the seven reference countries.

If new trials can be conducted, identify areas of R&D that would result in future indications, allowing a higher price.

Pharmacoeconomic evidence is also helpful and should be developed using Phase III trials that compare the product to current and emerging standards of therapy.

Whether there is a prepared New Medicine Submission or not, the PMPRB will begin a review as soon as it has notification of the first sale of the drug. It is far better to be proactive and prepare a strong rationale up front than it is to recover from a possibly negative reaction by the PMPRB reviewers.

Pharmacoeconomics

In Canada, 95% of pharmaceutical products are either fully or partially covered by third-party payors (e.g. private insurers, hospitals). In most cases, there also is already a pricing precedent for specific therapeutic areas. As a result, market access is highly dependent on providing proof of the cost/benefit ratio of a new product. Below are recommendations to consider when considering pharmacoecocomics.

Historically, most pharmacoeconomic data has been collected during Phase IV post-marketing clinical trials. While this does allow for more regional cost comparisons, it can also cause delays in formulary acceptance.

Including cost parameters in Phase III trials is an excellent proactive market access strategy; however, it is not always possible to include the scientific and economic goals.

Cost-benefit assessments are relative measurements. If the decision has been made to conduct only placebo-controlled Phase III Trials, the relative cost of using a new product versus a competitor's cannot be objectively established. Payors clearly prefer comparative clinical data.

Recruit one or more epidemiologists familiar with formulary requirements to assist the clinical team with the economic components of the protocol. The most valuable pharmacoeconomic studies are done using the key competitor against which you will position your drug at launch. Make sure that the pharmacoeconomic report will be easily understandable; most private payors do not have scientific reviewers.

Pharmacoeconomics analyses should not be included if:
- The Phase III trial requires any procedures that fall outside routine testing.
- Inclusion/exclusion criteria are very stringent so that cost applications cannot be applied across all patient categories.
- It appears that the economic components may jeopardize the scientific validity of the trial.
- The economic component cannot be customized to address regional cost issues.

Third-Party Payors

Third-party, private payors in Canada represent approximately 50% of the market. Many of them have unrestricted policies regarding the inclusion of new drugs and customize their programs for large employers and unions. Many private drug plans have generic substitution policies, and about 70% of the private plans have co-pays or deductibles.

Private payors need to be informed about the new product prior to the launch so that the launch team can become familiar with its submission requirements. Some payors require the NOC, product monograph and a clinical overview; others may require a more formal submission.

Understanding a payor's submission requirements is imperative to expedite the approval process for each payor.

The New Medicine Submission is the company's best opportunity to influence the pricing outcome for the new product. Some companies ignore the need for a New Medicine Submission, but for launch success, this opportunity cannot be overlooked. Presenting a submission with a strong rationale for the proposed product listing can help achieve the target price.

Common Drug Review

The CDR conducts clinical and cost-effectiveness evaluations of drugs and provides recommendations to "list" or "do not list" to provincial formularies (except in Quebec). Although created to eliminate the duplication of drug evaluations, many provinces continue to perform this drug evaluation function.

The average CDR approval rate "to list" is less than 50%. However a "do not list" recommendation translates to a "maybe" in several provinces if the recommendation is based on cost-effectiveness. The CDR also gives manufacturers an opportunity to revise their pricing during the embargo period (twenty days), which will be the price available to all participating plans. The manufacturer can address this issue through either CDR reconsideration or a product listing agreement at the provincial level.

Provincial Formulary

Each provincial formulary operates slightly differently, but each essentially has an initial staff group and a committee that reviews New Product Submissions and recommends to list or not list a product. Most formularies will accept submissions only after they are reviewed by the CDR. These committees are made up of practising clinicians, pharmacologists, pharmacists and economists, most of whom are also involved in private practice or academia. Although it may be possible to find proper ways to keep them informed of the science and competitive aspects of the new product, attempts to influence these people are discouraged. In fact, in some jurisdictions, committee members may need to declare a conflict if they have had contact with a manufacturer of a product that is up for review.

At twelve months pre-NOC, the team will have met with key staff in each provincial formulary department (preferably Drug Program Managers) to inform them of the upcoming launch. Now, at six months pre-NOC, continue to seek their guidance on pricing, value proposition, timing of submission and the potential for rapid or concurrent CDR review. Keep in touch with these key contacts to inform them of progress as NOC approaches. Make a list of all provincial and hospital formulary reimbursement committees and identify the key committee members.

Seek out occasions where these people will be accessible, such as professional association meetings, medical and pharmacy conferences, grand rounds, etc. and plan to have a company presence.

Every province has its own formulary of drugs that have been approved for reimbursement. To gain reimbursement, a separate submission is required for each province. Furthermore, each province has established its own criteria for submissions considered to be complete. It is critical to understand the requirements, deadlines and submission formats because these differences can mean months of delay, even with minor errors. Additionally, most provinces or professional associations have established clinical practice guidelines for various conditions, which can affect formulary inclusion. Accordingly, examine each individual province's criteria for priority listing, restricted or limited use, risk-sharing agreements, managed benefits, etc.

Create relationships with key stakeholders in the patient advocacy community. Patient access to drugs, public policy advocacy and issue management are all opportunities to build relationships with like-minded organizations. It is extremely helpful to build coalitions or to belong to partnerships on issues that forward the product.

As with PMPRB, the web sites for provincial formularies are excellent sources of information regarding the development of drug product submissions.

The following table lists some websites for provincial drug plans.

Table 12: Provincial drug plan websites

Province	Website
British Columbia Pharmacare	www.hlth.gov.bc.ca/pharme/drugsub.html
Alberta Health Drug Benefit List	www.health.gov.ab.ca/Drugs/index.htm
Saskatchewan Formulary	http://formulary.drugplan.health.gov.sk.ca
Manitoba Drug Benefits and Interchangeability Formulary	www.gov.mb.ca/health/mdbif/index.html
Ontario Drug Benefit Formulary	www.health.gov.on.ca/english/providers/ program/drugs/odbf_eformulary.html
Quebec Liste de Médicaments Assurés	www.ramq.gouv.qc.ca/fr/professionnels/ listmed/lm_tdmf.shtml
New Brunswick Prescription Drug Program Formulary	www.gnb.ca/0212/en/index.htm
Nova Scotia Formulary Managed by Atlantic Blue Cross	www.gov.ns.ca/health/pharmacare/formulary.asp
Prince Edward Island Formulary	www.gov.pe.ca/health/index. php3?number=1026181&lang=E
Newfoundland Interchangeable Drug Products Formulary	www.gov.nl.ca/health/nlpdp

A submission is no longer the end of the story at the provincial level. Once a committee has made a decision, the real work begins. Relationships that Market Access professionals have built within the drug program department are critically important during the next stage: the negotiation of the listing agreement.

In 2006, Product Listing Agreements (PLAs) were introduced in Ontario. The executive officer of the Ontario Drug Program can now list a product with the exceptional powers of that station. Even a drug that has had a negative "Do Not List" recommendation from CDR and a negative review from Ontario's Committee to Evaluate Drugs (CED) can lead to a subsequent pricing agreement with the province and a "General Benefit" listing on the public formulary. If the price is right and the province feels it has achieved savings for the drug program, the product will be listed on the formulary. Provincial jurisdictions that currently include PLAs as part of the listing negotiation process are Ontario, Manitoba, Alberta (July 2010) and British Columbia. Atlantic Canada and federal formularies (such as NIHB and RCMP) are rumoured to not be far behind.

Hospital Formulary

In general, the content of a Hospital Formulary submission is similar to that of a provincial drug formulary. You must demonstrate clinical efficacy, safety and cost-effectiveness. Some hospitals may request different types of data, depending on their specializations, which is determined on a case-by-case basis.

A standard hospital formulary submission package should be developed for the P&T (Pharmacy and Therapeutics) Committee review. Often the best way to deliver the hospital formulary package is through the regional or local sales representative. Ideally, the representative will have a relationship within the hospital setting. He or she should have a good relationship with the hospital pharmacist responsible for the formulary committee and should also know the influential clinicians on the review team. Each important individual on the P&T Committee should have a complete package of information. Usually, any physician in the hospital can bring a product to the attention of the P&T committee. Note that manufacturers cannot make a drug submission; it must come from a member of hospital staff, usually the head pharmacist.

Hospitals function independently, and decisions to list drugs on the formulary can happen much quicker than with provincial formularies. Also, because hospitals are considered independent units, pricing can be negotiated at a different level than that of the provincial formularies.

Hospital formulary committees usually prefer to receive submissions in three-ring binders, along with an electronic version on a thumb drive or CD-ROM.

Make sure to include the following information in your core submission package:
- Product Overview.
- Product Monograph.
- Product benefits and advantages in the hospital setting.
- Competitive comparisons, especially to the current standard of therapy.
- All pivotal clinical trial reprints, each with a one-page highlights overview.
- Special instructions related to the use of the product if it changes their standard of care.
- An unlocked Budget Impact Analysis (BIA) that allows the P&T to determine incremental costs/savings to the institution.
- Product ordering information, packaging, pricing, quantities and return policy.
- Other resources available, such as web sites and company contact names.

Key Activities 2–3 Months Prior to NOC

- Submission preparation for CDR and any provinces that may have concurrent review.
- Seek permission from provinces to have concurrent CDR review.
- Product price confirmation from PMPRB.
- Information sharing with Provincial drug program managers.
- Private payor administrators.
- Prioritized list of Hospital Formularies or buying groups. Report on status of Provincial, Third-party and Hospital Formulary packages.
- All completed and ready for final additions.
- Feedback from early communications with review boards and committees.
- Anticipated reactions to the new product.
- Prioritize and contact key stakeholders (patient groups, coalition, partnerships).
- Pre-NOC EMR drug listing activities.

Status of New Medicine Submission

- Timing of submission.
- PMPRB Category as requested.
- Pricing.
- Any preliminary feedback from the reviewers.

Day of NOC

- Letters mailed to drug plan managers (public and private) notifying them of NOC.
- Submission sent to CDR if product has not received a "priority review" designation for pre-NOC review.
- Quebec submission and other provinces.

Market Research Requirements Overview

Market Research Requirements for an NCE or Line Extension Launch are provided in this section.

Product Opportunity Assessment

Perform a product opportunity assessment to obtain a 360-degree view of the market opportunity.

Tasks to Complete

Complete a comprehensive competitive review of the market including:
- Secondary prescription and sales market analysis (IMS CompuScript, CDH, Brogan data).
- Rx by specialty group (to determine which specialists, if any, play an active role in the market).
- Current treatment of algorithms by indication.
- Current reimbursement landscape.
- Competitive intelligence on key competitors including patent and promotion information.
- Future competitors.
- Review and selection of best analogues for forecasting purposes.
- Preliminary qualitative opportunity assessment research with prescribers (small sample of relevant specialties) and KOLs:
  a. Identify trends in customer attitudes and behaviours in the market.
  b. Document perceived strengths and weaknesses of existing products/therapies.
  c. Identify existing unmet or emerging needs in the market (patient, physician and payor).
  d. Obtain customer reaction to preliminary product concept.

Developing the Opportunity

Continue the momentum of the initial product opportunity assessment in order to determine ideal product positioning, as well as potential barriers to product adoption.

Tasks to Complete

- Ongoing competitive intelligence on key competitors and issues in the market.
- Ongoing market trend tracking (Rx and sales market analysis). Including: market size, performance, composition, competitive mix and penetration.
- Existing and potential competitive activity.
- Regulatory, pricing and market access issues.
- Provincial formulary monitoring.
- Establishment of framework for required pre-launch market development activities.
- Development of framework for forecasting scenarios.
- Primary Market research:
    a. Comprehensive Qualitative Market Research: To establish preliminary positioning concepts, identify any behavioural barriers to prescribing and gain a comprehensive understanding of the market dynamics. This research should occur in several markets and be a large sample.
    b. Comprehensive Quantitative Market Research: To understand market dynamics, usage and attitude, an assessment is needed, which may include segmentation and one or more customer groups).

Preparing to Launch

The objective is to set the foundation of a successful launch.

Tasks to Complete

As performed while developing the opportunity, continue ongoing competitive intelligence on key competitors and issues in the market, as well as ongoing market trend tracking (Rx and sales market analysis).

Monitor key pre-launch market development activities (such as CME events and conferences).

- Product positioning development and refinement research.
- Development workshops with key specialists.
- Qualitative positioning evaluation and refinement research (with prescribers and, if needed, patients and patient advocacy groups).
- Pricing Sensitivity Research – if required.
- Qualitative Market Research – promotional development and testing.
- Concept development workshops (if required).
- Creative material testing (such as journal ads, detail aids, value-addition and patient materials).
- Establish pre-launch baselines for leading indicators of product performance.

Launch Assessment

Track launch performance and complete any research necessary for positioning and messaging adjustments.

Tasks to Complete

- Perform secondary data source monitoring of product performance tracking on key performance indicators including:
- Market growth, market penetration and share (total dollars and number of prescriptions).

- Competitor activity and response to new product launch.
- Regulatory, pricing and reimbursement issues.
- Variances to forecast and budget on key indicators.
- Quantitative post-detailing research with customers to assess detailing and message effectiveness.
- Quantitative post-launch monitoring research with customers (prescribers and patients).
- Components to include:
  a. Measurement of product awareness, trial and usage.
  b. Measurement of product satisfaction and performance against expectation and competitive set on key attributes/ behavioural drivers.
  c. Identification of perceived product strengths, weaknesses and competitive differentiation.
  d. Qualitative research among prescribers and non-prescribers (physicians) to:
  e. Identify key barriers to trial and usage among non-prescribers.
  f. Explore opportunities to leverage perceived strengths among prescribers with non-prescribers.
  g. Qualitative promotional material development and testing (if required).
  h. Evaluate new creative material (such as journal ads, detail aids, value-addition and patient materials) and key message refinements with customers (physicians and patients).

Tracking Product Performance

Support the continued success of the brand via regular performance tracking metrics and current and future opportunity analysis.

Tasks to Complete

Perform continual secondary data source monitoring of product performance tracking on key performance indicators, as one done in the launch assessment.

- Market growth, market penetration and share (total dollars and number of prescriptions).
- Competitor activity and response to new product launch.
- Regulatory, pricing and reimbursement issues.
- Variances to forecast and budget on key indicators.
- Ongoing competitive intelligence on key competitors and issues in the market, including new competitive entries and activities.
- Quantitative usage and attitude and market dynamics research with customers (prescribers and patients).
- Monitor satisfaction levels and product performance on leading indicators (awareness, trial and usage of new and total Rx), performance attributes and behavioural drivers) versus key competitors.
- Monitor perceived product strengths, weaknesses and areas of competitive differentiation.
- Identify unmet needs and emerging trends in the market that will affect perceptions and usage.
- Qualitative promotional material development and testing, as needed.
- Monitor Electronic Medical Records (EMR) regional and national drug database listing status.
- Market Research Requirements for the Acquisition of Marketed Drugs.
- Perform a comprehensive market review. Work with the cross-functional brand team to complete a comprehensive view of the market, including:

a. Prescription and sales market analysis.
b. Current treatment algorithms by indication.
c. Current reimbursement landscape.
d. Competitive intelligence on key competitors including patents and promotion information, if possible.
e. Identification of future competitors.
f. Data gap analysis.
- Identification of current secondary data gaps:
  a. What data resources do we need to obtain or subscribe to in order to compete in this market?
  b. What data is available from the original company?
- Identify primary market research data gaps:
  a. Obtain all historical primary market research.
  b. Identify any primary research opportunities identified during the completion/presentation of Part 1 (comprehensive market review).
- Identify key performance indicators and performance tracking metrics. Work with the cross-functional brand team to establish ongoing performance metrics. Develop product performance dashboard to track the above identified metrics.
- Continued primary and secondary market research support.
- Qualitative market research – exploring new opportunities and indications, performing creative and concept testing.
- Quantitative market research – detail tracking (detail and message effectiveness), such as through usage and awareness (U&A) studies. U&A studies measure the target audience's usage and awareness of a product. During the market research interview, the participant is typically asked if they are aware of products to treat a specific disease. Similarly, participants are asked which products they use to treat a specific disease and this contributes to usage of the product within the target audience.

Pharmaceutical Advertising Advisory Board (PAAB)

The PAAB mandate is to review advertising and promotional systems (APS) for approved pharmaceutical products. However, PAAB recognizes the importance of product launch timelines, and in this guideline, clarifies procedures for advertising review before Notice of Compliance (NOC) has been granted.

Prior to NOC, when the Product Monograph negotiations with the Therapeutic Products Directorate (TPD) have reached the final-draft stage, the advertiser or its agency may contact the PAAB to arrange a pre-NOC review of advertising and promotional systems.

PAAB accommodates pre-NOC submissions at the discretion of the PAAB Commissioner, with respect to workload at the time of submission, and will not be subject to the standard turnaround time.

Only core APS should be submitted for pre-NOC review. The number of core APS is limited to two and must be submitted at the same time. These APS should contain most of the proposed claims of the campaign. Submitting only the core APS at this stage can save the advertiser effort, time and money by avoiding the need to make the same revisions in multiple APS and re-submitting them several times. If necessary, PAAB will determine which APS are considered to be core. The APS requires approval by the advertiser's medical/regulatory staff prior to PAAB review.

Meetings between the advertiser and PAAB are not required for every product launch. Reasons for a meeting include: first in a new therapeutic class, new indication for existing product, novel marketing methods, competitive environment, complex pharmacology issues, cost-effectiveness issues, and ethical issues. The advertiser may contact PAAB to determine whether a meeting would be appropriate.

While waiting for the final approval of the Product Monograph, the company should apply PAAB revision requests to all the items that form the launch campaign.

When the pharmaceutical company receives its NOC, they should resubmit the final revised core APS, along with the NOC and Product Monograph (formal, written PAAB acceptance cannot be provided until the signed NOC and final Product Monograph are received). The advertiser should highlight additional revisions that may have been made to facilitate the review process. At this time, other launch APS may be submitted for PAAB review in one package.

After the launch campaign has been reviewed and accepted, any additional APS for the product will be processed within the customary PAAB procedure and timelines.

This guideline is effective January 1, 2003.

Regulatory Affairs (RA) & Quality Assurance (QA) Overview

RA is the central contact for all issues related to the registration of the product. It manages the development of the NDS, communications with TPD and negotiations related to product labelling. It is important to have excellent communications with RA colleagues so that they can understand the marketing strategy to create the best possible regulatory and pricing environment for the new product.

One of the most important aspects of the New Product Process is the area of technical due diligence. Very early in the process, QA assessments must be done on R&D development, chemistry and manufacturing data, production and scale-up reports, drug substance quality, etc. It may seem, at times, that QA is obstructing advancement; however, no matter how promising a new product may appear, if its development does not conform to very strict technical criteria, then it will not make it to market. Always include RA and QA in any team discussions related to the New Product Process.

Table 13 – Regulatory overview

LIFE CYCLE REGULATORY PLANNING	
Drugs Requiring Approval	**Approved Drugs**
Regulatory due diligence of licensee non-clinical and clinical CMC data and pending or ongoing clinical protocols for TPD approvability.	Attend regular project meetings for strategy.
Book and hold pre-NDS meeting with TPD for clinical program and submission guidance; recommend adjustments to program as required.	Submission to TPD to transfer, or cross-reference NOC to Strategic (n/a for distribution-only products).
Market Access: hold meetings with provincial payors and CDR to obtain guidance on potential approvability/coverage; adjustments to product program as required.	Redesign product labels to Strategic standards and new DINs, as applicable.
Attend regular project meetings for updates on aspects that may impact filing.	Transfer Pharmacovigilance activities and all regulatory files to Strategic as applicable.
Earliest preparation of submission (NDS/SNDS); interaction with licensee, manufacturing, QA as required for documents (Strategic or licensee).	Revise product monograph and product labelling to Strategic trade dress and Med Info contact number.
Create draft product monograph in conjunction with Marketing and Market Access (and licensee).	Review and update advertising and promotional materials, and incorporate Strategic address and Med Info number as applicable via DCR process (in conjunction with marketing).
Earliest possible NDS filing (target 345 days review for new product submission).	Update/create medical letters (Med Info.).

Upon acceptance for review (45 days), provide relevant NDS/SNDS sections to Market Access for formulary submission preparation.	
Timely response to TPD queries during review to support target NOC date.	
Eight months prior to NOC date, assist in creation and finalization of product labelling (container, carton, as applicable) in conjunction with Marketing and Labelling.	
Forward DINs to labelling department as soon as available (approximately two weeks prior to NOC). Goal to have container labels printed one day after DIN release for immediate launch product labelling and "date of first sale" for timely formulary submissions.	
Provide copy of NOC and "date of first sale" document to Market Access for inclusion in CDR, Quebec, and private payor formulary submissions. Complete and file DNF after first sale.	

Strategy Development

Key Elements of a Commercial Assessment

The following is an overview of a commercial assessment and the associated content to include in a commercial plan. The lists are not exhaustive, but serve as a quick reference guide. When completing each section of a commercial assessment, create a summary of the most significant findings.

The business review is an annual, ongoing process completed by the product manager that begins when a molecule is discovered and continues until a product is discontinued. While conducting a thorough business review may not be as exciting as developing a new advertising campaign, a good plan cannot be created without the due diligence applied to the review. The business review leads to a robust SWOT analysis, identification of key issues, accurate and robust description of strategic imperatives, sustainable positioning, and the appropriate tactics to support your strategic initiatives.

- Executive Summary.
- Introduction.
- Business Review: Disease, Product and Market.
- Crafting Brand Strategy.
- Pricing and Reimbursement Strategy.
- Customer Strategy.
- Forecasting Assumptions.
- Marketing Goals: Key Metrics.
- Tactical Plan.
- Sales Force Plan.
- Conducting financial forecasts: Forecast (5-10 year).
- Brand P&L Statement.
- Market Research Plan.
- Life Cycle Management Planning.

Key Elements of a Launch Plan

- Executive Summary.
- Introduction: IP, trademarks, branding, naming, deal terms, patent life.
- A comprehensive Business Review: recommendations, conclusions, gaps, trends, priorities.
- Disease.
- Product.
- Market Definition.

- Pricing and reimbursement.
- SWOT (power rank).
- Key issues (rationale) and partner challenges if relevant.
- Strategic imperatives.
- Marketing Strategies.
- Customer Strategy: Segmentation/Targeting Strategy.
- Positioning suggestions (based on initial qualitative market research).
- Key selling messages.
- Promotional strategy.
- Sales force size analysis.
- Market research plan/gaps identified.
- Pricing options/recommendation (considering PMPRB, formulary access challenges).
- Financials (P&L), Budgets.
- Promotional investment required: 3–5 years.
- Life cycle planning considerations: additional indications.
- Forecast scenarios including life cycle opportunities:
  a. Dollars and units.
- Key Assumptions.
- Pre-launch tactical plan.
- Launch tactical plan.
- Launch Timeline and short-term and long-term launch metrics.

Training Overview

This section is intended to provide guidelines of the process of preparation for a new product launch.

This document will take the Training Manager through the process from when a new product is announced internally to the launch of a product in the Canadian marketplace.

Target audience includes Sales Representatives, Sales Managers, National Sales Director, Key Account Managers, Business Unit Directors, Product Manager, Medical Information, Reimbursement Manager.

The timelines for the Training Plan are outlined below. Generally, this process may take be between 4–6 months.

Stage 1: Training Plan Development

The training plan for any new product should take between 30–45 days. During this stage you will develop a tactical training plan based on the proposed launch date of the product. You should identify and work with external and internal resources, as well as key stakeholders, that will have an impact on the brand. The steps of stage 1 are as follows:

1. Gathering Market Intelligence – working closely with the brand team or new product development, it is important to gather any and all information with respect to the disease state, the therapeutic area, treatment options and the positioning of potential competitors should they exist. All information that is available regarding the new product should also be compiled, as it will be required in the next steps. There are no monetary costs associated with this stage.

2. Training Plan Creation Consultation – consulting with the brand team and the National Sales Director, it is important to prepare a tactical Training Plan that supports the overall Brand Strategy. This will be a starting point for future training. The document you create is a living document and will likely change as time progresses throughout the launch process.

3. Creation of a Strategic Overview – once you have identified the needs required by the brand team and National Sales Director, with the market intelligence compiled, it is important to develop a

Strategic Overview. This can be one page document designed for the company executive highlighting the Training Strategy. The document should contain your high level training objectives.

4. Existing Material Review –there may already be existing, training material and clinical data that can be obtained internally or from other countries where the product has been approved. You should review this information prior to the next steps.

5. Creation of the Tactical Plan – once the overall Training Strategy has been developed and approved by the Business Unit Director, a tactical plan will be necessary in order to identify all the steps that will be implemented to achieve the ultimate objective outlined in the Strategic Overview.

6. Brand Team Approval –plan a meeting to present the Strategic and Tactical Plans to the Brand Team for their input. Another meeting may be required for final approval once all edits are made and approved by the Leadership team.

7. Leadership Approval – submit the Strategic and Tactical Plans to the Leadership team for review and approval. Once this has been completed, vendor pitches can be organized.

8. Vendor Selection – based on the Training Plan, it must be decided which aspects of the plan can be developed in house and which will require external support. The following factors should be considered: internal resource expertise, scope of the project, translation requirements/timelines, internal staff qualification, as well as time to complete the project. For example, Self-study Product Training Module content is extremely time-consuming to develop to ensure it aligns with the Brand Strategy. Medical writers and instructional designers will be required. Consistency is important, and should there be multiple tactics (i.e. self-study, pre-launch and launch),

you must consider the advantages of one vendor vs. multiple vendors and how it supports the strategy. It is important to assess each vendor based on experience with: your company, in the pharmaceutical industry, and in the therapeutic area, as well as its present portfolio, understanding of Strategic Culture philosophy and cost. You should meet with vendors to outline your training plan and needs, then they will return with proposals. Procurement has preferred vendors in certain areas and also has agencies of record for marketing activities. Consult with your Business Unit Director if there are preferred training agencies. You should also consult Procurement to ensure an inclusive selection process. If there is no training agency of record you should meet with 2–3 vendors to ensure that you hire the company which will provide you with the best service that meets your needs.

Stage 2: Training Program Development

The second stage in training for a new product launch is the development of the Training Program. Based on the strategies established in the Training Plan, the Training Program(s) must be developed to meet the goals of Stage 1. During this stage the Training Team will work closely with both internal and external partners. These partners will be highlighted in each section of the Training Program Development. The process must have all functional areas aligned to the overall objectives and work to achieve those goals. The timeline for this portion of the launch, based on a new product to the Canadian market, is 120–150 days.

1. Product and Disease Knowledge (PDK) Study Material Development – you develop the home study materials that will be used primarily by Sales Representatives and Regional Sales Managers. In your Training Plan, you will have decided whether home study will be paper-based, online through a Learning Management or e-Learning platform (LMS) or a blend.

Your vendor will provide medical writing and adult learning principles to apply to your projects. You will be in constant contact with these individuals and your brand team during this step. Study material will encompass all disease state knowledge, therapeutic knowledge, treatment options, product information, competitive knowledge and possibly product messages based on positioning (product messaging may not happen until the actual Launch Meeting), with associated testing. All study material will need to be approved by your medical group for accuracy and referencing review. The cost associated with PDK development can vary depending on how you chose to roll it out. If paper-based, the cost can be approximately $65,000, depending on how much writing and formatting has to be done. If online, cost can range from $100,000 to $250,000, depending on the elements incorporated.

2. Develop Online Product Testing – if testing engine does not exist, you may need to work with IT and an external vendor to create this engine or use an existing engine provided by your vendor.

3. Product Monograph Materials –you will work closely with the regulatory department to ensure that you have the most up-to-date copy of the Product Monograph. A physical copy of the Product Monograph is usually sent out with the study modules or in electronic form as part of the home study.

4. Clinical Paper Materials – clinical papers are for background purposes only, unless marketing deems it necessary to use one or more as a promotional piece. Clinical papers associated with the product will be purchased and sent out to the representatives and any other applicable parties with all other study materials. An online test associated with these papers will be developed, if necessary, at a later step. This will take approximately ten days to build, plus translation time for test questions.

5.   Launch Meeting Workshop Development – launch Meeting workshops need to be developed that are highly interactive, allowing the participants to demonstrate knowledge gained in the Home Study as well as application of the selling messages and support tools. Your vendor will be an excellent partner in developing these workshops. You will need to determine how many workshop leaders will be needed.

6.   Pre-Launch Training – the next step in launching a new product will be to develop a pre-launch training program, as well as workshops that can carry over to the launch meeting. It is important to create continuity between the pre-launch training and the launch meeting. An outside vendor with expertise in workshop development and learning principles can be used should you not have that knowledge internally. If using an external vendor, this process takes a minimum of 90 days and can cost from $40,000–$150,000.

7.   Final Training Review – upon completion of the above steps, a final run through with the Leadership Team and the Brand Team will be conducted to get approval and feedback on any adjustments that may need to be made to the training programs. Once this is complete and adjustments have been made, the next step of training roll-out and launch readiness can begin.

Stage 3:
Training Roll-Out and Launch Readiness

The final training step is to roll out the training program to internal employees, Regional Sales Management team and the Sales Force. Home Study materials have been approved and ready. All presentations and workshops are ready and approved. This stage should take place over a period of approximately 90 days.

1. Marketing POA (Plan of Action) Presentation – this is an opportunity to create excitement and alignment around the new brand. The Launch Brand Team will present the Brand Plan to the rest of the organization. The Training Team will participate with a prepared presentation on the training plan.

2. RSM/KAM Training Communication – Regional Sales Management (RSM) team should receive training prior to the sales representatives. KAMs may or may not be included in this process, depending on the level of activity they have with the brand. Initially it is important to send out materials these managers may need for home study purposes, accompanied by the appropriate communication of what to expect in their materials, timelines for training and details about their travel to the head office for training. Typically there will be a managers meeting prior to the Launch Meeting, where the RSM team will have the opportunity to work with the marketing material and be informed about the details of the launch meeting, including their roles.

3. Pre-Training Communication/Assignment and Sales Force Home Study – approximately 6–8 weeks prior to the launch meeting, a communication should be sent to the sales force with details about its home study assignments, testing and pre-launch training meetings. A second communication from the Leadership Team should be sent regarding the launch meeting, with details surrounding that meeting and any associated travel. Depending on the depth of material to be studied, representatives should be given 15–20 business days to complete their home study assignments and testing. Time away from their territory should be minimally affected by this home study; minimal passing grades should be established for the online testing. Usual passing grades vary from 80–90%.

4. Pre-launch Training – with the high costs needed to bring representatives to a central location for additional training, alternative options are available. Consider frequent Web-ex sessions for the home study period to solidify the learning process, using internal subject matter experts.

5. Launch Meeting – the launch meeting is where it all comes together. You will need to work closely with all internal stakeholders. The purpose of the meeting is to create excitement around the brand and ensure that the sales force is ready to meet with customers and deliver the messaging while using the appropriate tools. The role of the Training Manager is to create workshops that stimulate the excitement and ensure message mastery skills by the representatives. The cost of this meeting is usually absorbed by the sales and marketing departments. Daily meeting evaluations should be performed.

ACKNOWLEDGEMENTS

A resource book like this is not possible without the assistance, guidance and co-operation of many individuals.

Among those who have supported my efforts are Jordan Delanghe, Azeem Gill, Liisa Vexler, Rui Paiva, Michael Milloy, Richard O'Daiskey, Janet Shaw, Joe Van Troost, Dave Solomon, Andrea Mulder, Don Swainson, Lindsay Williams, Kristina Murphy, Marguerite Zimmerman, Steve Barrett, Vijay Sappani, Michel Theriault, Aran Amaral and Kristen Clancy.

My gratitude to all and to anyone I may have inadvertently left out.

ABOUT THE AUTHOR

David Bard is an entrepreneur, business leader, marketing consultant, speaker and author. He has nearly 20 years of leadership experience in pharmaceutical and medical device marketing, sales, and training and has worked with leading healthcare companies across North America. His expertise is borne out of more than a dozen successful launches. Dave's passion is launching new products and delves into new product development, brand management, lifecycle management planning, sales management and product management training, as well as commercialization experience in more than 20 therapeutic areas.

As an expert product launch marketer, Bard developed a launch system that clearly identifies a comprehensive process for a successful launch to escalate a company's performance and to ensure launch success.

His company, Pharma Launch Inc. was founded to address a gap in the marketplace that he identified: companies of all sizes have few processes in place for new product commercialization. Without a clear and comprehensive new product process, a company is left to guess on many aspects of a new product launch, with millions of dollars sometimes at stake.

Dave eventually transitioned to consulting for life science companies to assist launch teams in their preparation and assessments of product launches. He wrote *Launch: Life Sciences Products* to share his knowledge and passion for launching life sciences products.

When not at work, Dave is a karate teacher, home renovator and world traveler. His favourite time spent is sitting with family and friends by the campfire or drinking his ritual morning coffee in the outdoors.

Pharma Launch Inc.

Pharma Launch Inc. is a strategic marketing and training consultancy specializing in improving product launch performance in the life sciences industry. We know that all product launches are unique and at times complex. We also believe that a successful product launch means your product is reaching more patients. Our aim is to help your company make your next launch even better than your last launch. More product reaching patients means more patients benefiting from treatment, which is your company's ultimate goal.

When you are ready for your best launch yet, visit www.PharmaLaunch.ca to schedule your complementary diagnostic conversation.

On-line Launch Process Diagnostics

Pharma Launch offers a free launch diagnostics service to help marketers assess their company's launch process and compare it to the average industry launch.

By completing a ten-minute survey, you can determine how your company's product launch performance capabilities compare to those of an aggregation of life sciences companies.

The results of the diagnostics will be e-mailed to you along with instructions on how to improve and address the gaps in your launch process.

Visit www.**PharmaLaunch.Guru** to learn more.

CPSIA information can be obtained at www.ICGtesting.com
Printed in the USA
LVOW04s0636080715

445325LV00016B/144/P